W9-AQM-692

FORAGED FLAVOR

FINDING FABULOUS INGREDIENTS
IN YOUR BACKYARD OR FARMER'S MARKET

FORAGED FLAVOR

TAMA MATSUOKA WONG WITH EDDY LEROUX
FOREWORD BY DANIEL BOULUD

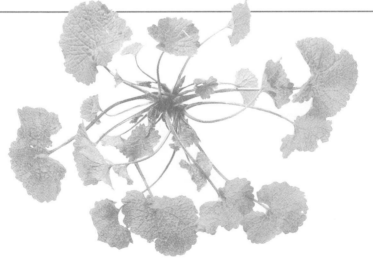

CLARKSON POTTER PUBLISHERS
NEW YORK

NRC   CASS COUNTY PUBLIC LIBRARY
       400 E. MECHANIC
       HARRISONVILLE, MO 64701

       0 0022 0417572 9

It is the responsibility of the reader to identify and correctly use the edible plants described in this book. The authors and publisher assume no responsibility for any adverse effects that may result from the reader's misidentification or incorrect use of such edible plants.

Copyright © 2012 by Tama Matsuoka and Eddy Leroux
Photographs copyright © 2012 by Thomas Schauer–Studio for Photography LLC
Illustrations copyright © 2012 by Kate McKeon

All rights reserved.
Published in the United States by Clarkson Potter/Publishers, an imprint of the Crown Publishing Group, a division of Random House, Inc., New York.
www.crownpublishing.com
www.clarksonpotter.com

CLARKSON POTTER is a trademark and POTTER with colophon is a registered trademark of Random House, Inc.

Library of Congress Cataloging-in-Publication Data
Wong, Tama Matsuoka.
    Foraged flavor : finding fabulous ingredients in your back-yard or farmer's market, with 88 recipes / Tama Matsuoka Wong with Eddy Leroux ; foreword by Daniel Boulud.
        p. cm.
    (hardback)
1. Cooking (Wild foods)   2. Cooking, American.   3. Wild plants, Edible.   I. Leroux, Eddy.   II. Title.
    TX823.W65 2012
    581.6'32—dc23   2011036334

ISBN 978-0-307-95661-3
eISBN 978-0-307-95662-0
Printed in the United States of America

Book design by Marysarah Quinn
Jacket design by Marysarah Quinn
Jacket photographs by Thomas Schauer

10   9   8   7   6   5   4   3   2   1

FIRST EDITION

TO OUR FAMILIES

What would the world be, once bereft
Of wet and of wildness?
Let them be left,
O let them be left, wildness and wet;
Long live the weeds and the wilderness yet.

— GERARD MANLEY HOPKINS

I believe a leaf of grass is no less than the journey-work of the stars,
And the pismire is equally perfect, and a grain of sand, and the egg of the wren,
And the tree-toad is a chef-d'oeuvre for the highest,
And the running blackberry would adorn the parlors of heaven . . .

—WALT WHITMAN

CONTENTS

FOREWORD

Foraging is about harvesting the wild, ephemeral, and rare flavors found in nature. As chefs, we're always looking for ingredients to inspire us in the kitchen. While many wonderful purveyors bring them to our door, Tama's herbs, flowers, and plants—many of which we discover through her for the first time—truly stand apart. We never know just what she'll have in her bulging bags!

On the farm outside Lyon where I was raised, we planned our plantings and their corresponding harvests carefully. Foragers take an utterly different approach, gathering what nature so preciously offers, often seemingly at whim. Few are as attuned to wilderness's hidden treasures as Tama. Her profound knowledge and years of dedication uncover a bounty that remains hidden to most of us. While you might not think of New York City and nature in the same breath, not far beyond our streetscapes lie beautiful mountains, streams, valleys—all ripe for foraging—and a climate with wonderfully distinct seasons. This is Tama's unpredictable world, one of modest yet magical harvests, gleaned by love and respect for the natural world.

Although foraging may not supply the main ingredients we use at my restaurants, it does offer up a wealth of inspiration for extraordinary talents like Eddy Leroux, the chef de cuisine at Daniel. Few could so ingeniously embrace cooking with the out-of-the-ordinary flavors and textures of foraged plants with such passion and interest. Eddy studies the profile of each wild plant, associating its flavors with familiar ones such as anise, celery, or cinnamon, and uses it as his springboard for creating something new.

I love being in the kitchen when Tama arrives. Her eyes sparkle with excitement as she spreads her foraged plants on the table and describes to Eddy how she climbed high in a tree or crouched low in a bush to pick an ingredient at just the right stage of its growth. She explains the way the plant grows and shares her knowledge while Eddy tastes. Sometimes I look over the plastic bags of herbs, still dewy from the outdoors, and ask him, "What will you do with that?" Then, before the kitchen gets impossibly busy with cooks prepping for dinner service, Eddy spends some quiet time experimenting.

I invite you to read on to savor Tama's passion for nature and Eddy's creativity as the two come together to offer you their extraordinary approach to food.

—DANIEL BOULUD

INTRODUCTION

When I am walking a wooded path on an early spring morning, the ground carpeted with wildflowers, I smell the dew and moist earth beneath me. On a summer evening, dusk falling, the breeze in my hair also bends the tall, vibrantly colored meadow wildflowers, and all else falls away.

It is not too much of a leap to go from the sensory experience of these smells and sights to their taste. Wild plants can have more kick than cultivated ones, which have been bred and cloned to give the same experience apple after apple, lettuce leaf after lettuce leaf. Although sometimes startling and sharp, a wild taste is often more complex, sweet and tart at the same time, with a symphony of flavors and notes. Similarly, wild plants look and act more like individuals, as they have not been airbrushed or altered to sit on a supermarket shelf like Hollywood stars. They are sometimes homely, with a blemish or two; their true beauty is in their internal character, not their outward appearance.

I now know what every single plant is in my meadow, creek bed, and forest—a complete botanical smorgasbord of more than two hundred wild plants. But a decade earlier, when my interest began in earnest, I could identify only two plants—oaks and dandelions. I started to tag along on wildflower and conservation group field tours, inviting the naturalists and botanists I met for tea afterward and peppering them with questions. Little by little, the pages in my field guides became more and more dog-eared; in the bathtub at the end of the day, I would review them, matching plants I'd seen to images in the book. I started really connecting with growers at farmer's markets; we would talk about the weather, about great produce, about crop pollinators. The quality of a landscape and the types of wild plants that grow there can tell you a lot about the quality of the food that unique piece of earth will produce.

It was pretty easy to find nature-oriented books that told me which of these plants are "edible," but my quest instead was for plants that actually taste *good*. The existing books offered recipes with instructions such as "parboil in water three times to remove bitterness" or "braise the milkweed shoots for two hours." It sounded too much like space shuttle or survival food—the kind of thing you'd eat only if you were starving in the wilderness! Others had information along the lines of "You can throw it into a salad or soup and you won't even taste it."

But I was looking for a way of working with these ingredients that would truly showcase them in a classic and balanced seasonal dish. To me this is the essence of the cooking of Daniel Boulud. I told myself that if the chefs at his flagship restaurant, Daniel, could not cook a plant into something tasty, I doubted if many others would be able to. But, if these sometimes unattractive but freely available ingredients could be appreciated by great restaurant chefs, then why not introduce them to home cooks, and let them in on a great secret?

Behind this cooking philosophy—that of highlighting the unique flavor of an ingredient—lies passion and intuition; there is the sensory explora-tion of a plant's taste and texture, the recollection of thousands of flavors in human culinary traditions, the ability to create a dish around a particular taste. The plant can be the star of a dish or it can join the family of flavors on the plate. And I have come to appreciate that Daniel's chef de cuisine, Eddy Leroux, has that streak of genius and the discipline to achieve this.

ANISE HYSSOP

In late June 2009, by chance and at the urging of friends—but with no introduction—I brought some anise hyssop (*Agastache foeniculum*) from my meadow garden to the receptionist at restaurant Daniel. I couldn't resist because the hyssop had looked so fresh and tempting that morning, and my husband and I had already been enjoying the crushed leaves to enhance a glass of Prosecco in the early summer evenings. I had a reservation later that night for dinner with friends. The receptionist called the kitchen and randomly inquired if the chefs could do something with anise hyssop. "Sure," was the answer, and that evening, voilà! We had added to our tasting menu two amazing dishes that showcased the herb's concentrated licorice flavor but not in an overpowering way: shrimp and melon with anise hyssop vinaigrette as a starter, and anise hyssop and yuzu sorbet as a dessert.

After dinner we retired to the kitchen to congratulate the contributing chefs: Eddy Leroux, chef de cuisine, and Dominique Ansel, executive pastry chef. Eddy asked me if I had other things in my meadow. I said, "Yes . . . what are you looking for?" He replied (and maybe he would later regret this), "Bring me everything!" and gave me his card.

That is how it started—with maybe a pinch of disbelief on either side (*Why is she bringing me stuff? Why is he creating recipes?*). And there we were, two people obsessed with food on the one hand and plants on the other.

Over the next year a routine developed. Every week when I was in New York City advising a Wall Street client at the firm's midtown trading floor, I would walk up the block and bring Eddy whatever had looked good earlier that day near my home in New Jersey. In particular, I liked to bring the kinds of plain plants that people tread on or walk by every day without noticing. As Eddy and I sat in the silent dining room before the restaurant came to life, an hour might fly by as we discussed, debated, and tasted my latest stash of wild edibles: where I had found each plant growing, when the peak season was, how much volume might be available depending on the weather, how long the plant would be around. If it was something new, I would bring him results of my research about how people in other cultures prepare and eat the plant. Sometimes it would take months of debate before he decided something I had found was in peak season and ripe for cooking. Then a period of testing followed— raw, sautéed, fried, braised, dried, infused. Other times he would astonish me, asking for a plant that I had dismissed as survival food but that he remembered eating a decade ago prepared in a way I had never imagined. And of course, the ultimate reward was enticing friends and business colleagues to meals at the restaurant to sample the latest successful discovery. There is nothing to compare with tasting something that you have plucked

STINGING NETTLE

from the earth transformed into a sublime meal.

Stinging nettle (*Urtica dioica*), for example, is a favorite, with a deep, green taste of spring and notes of celery and mint. I brought some in to the restaurant kitchen straight from a forest edge. Eddy loved it and asked me if I could start bringing in a larger supply, since it reduces greatly upon cooking. At first I scoffed at the idea of bringing in volumes of plant material on my commute but . . . somehow in May and June I found myself toting large garbage bags stuffed with stinging nettles along with my business papers for meetings in the city. The large bags attracted immediate interest from the security guards at the entrance to the commuter PATH trains. "Please stand to the side so we can inspect your garbage bag, Miss." When they grabbed the bags I warned them to watch out or they could "sting" themselves. They looked at me half in alarm at whether this was a potential security issue and, after gingerly opening a bag, shrugged on seeing that it contained only a bunch of weeds. "Have a nice day," they said and sent me on my way.

Next stop before the restaurant was the trading floor. I was a little tired of hauling the bags over my shoulder after my two-hour commute, so I was dragging them behind me on the trading floor. The traders smirked. "Bringing in your laundry? Or is that garbage?" No, I answered, refusing to divulge the mysterious contents. The business analysts couldn't resist gathering around and opening a bag; the trading desk area was immediately filled with an aroma that was thick, almost incense-like. "Don't touch!" I warned, and they shrank back, fearful. The British traders recognized the nettles right away, reminded of the English countryside hedgerows that are left to grow thick with brambles and nettles.

Eddy immediately pounced on the nettles, turning them into a foam to partner with a hazelnut-encrusted scallop dish at the restaurant. Soon after the nettles experience, I started spending less and less of my time on the trading floor and more of it lugging huge garbage bags of weeds across the city. I became obsessed with discovering new plants, with bringing in new tastes. Whenever I was driving around or riding on a bus, I couldn't help but search the passing landscapes for certain plants. I started asking my friends in London and France and my relatives in Japan to send me books on edible plants in their regions. My mind now associated images of plants with not just their species, genus, habitat, and season, but also their unique flavors. Eventually I quit taking on new financial services projects (at least during the foraging season) and became engaged full time in this new rich world of outdoor flavors.

I am having so much fun delving deep into the world of foraging and wild plants and slow food, giving talks and tours while continuing to attend talks and tours of others. Organic farmer's associations, beekeepers, gardeners, naturalists, chefs, and natural-foods grocers all have practical day-to-day experiences, questions, and challenges that are great to share and learn from. I especially collaborate with conservation groups, including New Jersey Audubon, New Jersey Conservation, my local Hunterdon County Land Trust, the Schuylkill Center, municipalities, and watershed organizations, in stewarding some of the lands they care for and in ferreting out invasive plants to help restore ecological balance to their preserves. I also have an arrangement with one of my local organic farmers who has lots of great weeds that I can explore for their culinary potential and that he can then selectively harvest to add to the offerings at his stand at the farmer's market. All these exchanges seem like the beginning of something—tastes of a larger movement to come.

For his part, Eddy, after twenty-five years of professional cooking, still gets excited about meeting new yet ancient ingredients, like a painter finding a new color. And because there are so many still undiscovered tastes, each season he looks forward both to old favorites and to some surprise gifts. I prod him to keep working on the unfamiliar items, even if at first nibble they taste strange or uninteresting. Instead of relying on a predictable core repertoire of tried-and-true dishes, he is always pushing himself, insatiably curious, trying to capture the indefinable essence of an ingredient, at the exact right time in the season. This culture and energy pervades the restaurant, for Daniel has an interest in everything—always peppering me with questions—and a mind like a steel trap. Whenever the season changes, the general manager, Pierre Siue, asks me to give seminars to the dining room staff so they can explain the plants to inquisitive diners. We're even planning to take the show on the road with a foraging bus trip for the cooks. Daniel gives us a window to explore these ingredients, to push ourselves—as he pushes himself and his team every day—and for Daniel's generosity and spirit we are grateful.

After tasting and testing many edible plants, sometimes the same ones harvested at different times of the year, we have many favorites. In this book, we profile our seventy-one winners, as judged by taste and accessibility; the vast majority of these plants are found across the entire country. If you choose to eat your way through the eighty-four recipes here over the course of four seasons, as we did, you can enjoy an average of a new plant a week for more than a year. Although Eddy is a professional chef, the recipes here are decidedly home-style ones that showcase the plants without using expensive ingredients, time-consuming cooking techniques—or a cadre of prep chefs. Instead they incorporate a chef's eye for color, texture, and taste, but are easy to prepare for everyday cooking. (In fact, my ninth grader, Georgia, whipped up a batch of the Amaranth and Feta Phyllo Triangles [page 166] on a weeknight as a treat for my publisher.) Eddy and I hope you and your friends and family find new favorites in here, as well as some reasons to get out and explore the great outdoors— or even your yard or a local farmer's market, where less intrepid foragers will find some of these very same ingredients.

BROADLEAF DOCK

ARALIA BUD

CARDAMINE

CHICKWEED

CURLY DOCK

DANDELION

CREEPING JENNY

DAYLILY SHOOT

FIELD MUSTARD

DEAD NETTLE

GARLIC PENNYCRESS

GARLIC MUSTARD

FRAGRANT BEDSTRAW

HENBIT

KNOTWEED

SHEEP SORREL

COMMON BLUE VIOLET

WILD GARLIC
SHOOTS

YELLOW ROCKET

SPRING

ARTEMISIA/
MUGWORT

CATTAIL

SPRUCE TIPS

STINGING NETTLE

WISTERIA

SUMMER

AMARANTH

ANISE HYSSOP

BEE BALM

DAYLILY
FLOWER AND BUDS

WILD GARLIC HEAD

ELDERFLOWER

SHAGGY SOLDIERS

ASIAN
HONEYSUCKLE

LAVENDER BERGAMOT

WILD SPEARMINT

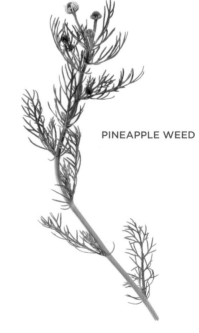

PINEAPPLE WEED

WILD ROSE

SHISO

WILD BLUEBERRY

YELLOW
WOOD SORREL

PURSLANE

LAMBSQUARTERS

JUNIPER

PAWPAW

WHITE PINE

SUMAC

WILD RAISIN

QUEEN ANNE'S LACE

BARBERRY

IN THE FIELD

For quite a while I didn't know that what I was doing was called foraging. The first time I heard the word was when Daniel once asked cheerfully, "How is foraging?" It made me feel slightly uneasy; I think I had it confused with "rummaging"—as in combing through secondhand furniture or clothing. It was only when my neighbor, who has been in the food business for decades, interrupted another one of my long ramblings (about finding *this* plant and cooking it *that* way) to say, gesturing emphatically, "You know what you are? You are a *forager*," that I learned that foraging was a thing—and a hot one at that.

So foraging is new, but it is also old and here to stay: It dates back to before farming, which is to say, before civilization. There are approximately 21,000 plants that grow wild (meaning without cultivation) in North America and 300,000 worldwide. Of these—and experts differ on the exact number—some 4,000 to 7,000 are known to be edible. Wild plants have long been gathered not only for sustenance but also as culinary treasures. Spices that we take for granted today on supermarket spice racks actually date back to foraged handfuls of herbs, seeds, and berries that were used to impart flavor and aroma to food centuries ago.

It is only in the last century that subsistence agriculture has given way to large-scale commercial food production on an international level, the cultivation of minor crops has declined, and—along with it—the knowledge of wild local foods has gradually become lost. In many industrialized nations today, typical food sources are limited to just twenty-five to sixty vegetables, fruits, and grains that are cultivated or imported. (You can guess them: corn, wheat, soybeans, tomatoes, potatoes, etc.) This constriction of the types of plants that we depend on for food also means a greater dependence on precious few crops that are potentially vulnerable to blight or weather events, such as drought or flood. Repeating this pattern, always farming the same few things on the same parcel of land, also depletes our soil of valuable nutrients and diverse organic matter. In comparison, a nine-inch-square patch of wild meadow can support as many as twenty different species, changing through the seasons. Even our palates suffer—many of our taste experiences are becoming limited to a generic set of flavors, dominated by bland, sweet, and starchy.

Adding a couple of wild foods to your table and introducing a diversity of plants in peak season is healthy and the way we are meant to eat. Researchers are finding that wild plants, consumed in regular portions when in season, are high in nutritional value. For example, purslane is one of the best sources of omega-3 and sumac is loaded with vitamin C. My family all remarked after we had finished foraging and testing most of the recipes in this cookbook that we felt healthier, with more energy and fewer allergies.

(There is a school of thought, largely anecdotal, that eating small amounts of pollen through local honey, plants, and flowers may introduce the substances to the body almost like a vaccine, so that the body's immune system no longer perceives them as hostile invaders and will not unleash a host of allergy symptoms to fight them off.) Somewhere along the way we also lost the urge to snack between meals, perhaps because we felt fuller.

But the main reason to forage is because it is fun and free. There's a sense of discovery, and for good reason: Unlike in a typical garden or farm crop, the wild plants growing on the same piece of earth can be magically changing every two weeks or so. When I am out in the field there is something deeply satisfying, a feeling of connection with a ritual that is at the root of human existence. In all seasons, walking, mucking about outside, looking at what is all around, and choosing what to gather are invigorating. After an hour or so, often with one or more of my daughters, we return home; our faces are flushed with the glow of fresh air in our lungs. We eat well and we sleep like logs.

FINDING AND IDENTIFYING WILD PLANTS

The first reaction many people have when they hear that I forage for wild plants is to ask if I have ever gotten sick. I haven't. Believe it or not, human brains are actually hardwired to remember plants visually and to distinguish them better than phone numbers, computer instructions, or standardized-test multiple-choice questions. That's not to say that foraging should be taken lightly, but the principles and tips for identifying plants that I outline in this book will help you enormously. Start with a handful of plants that you can learn to recognize easily, and little by little add on. Purslane and lambs-quarters, for example, which are often found at farmer's markets, are great contenders. Another good plant to begin with is wild garlic. It is easy to identify, find, and cook a dozen ways. Other great starter plants are dande-lion, wisteria, the yellow mustards, sumac, and pine needles.

Of course, some plants are easier to identify than others, and some entire plant families (like mint and mustard) are not only edible but also tasty and nutritious. Yet, in most cases, it is still important to identify the plant down to the species level by the Latin name. Common names often vary by time and place and may be based on local custom, whereas the Latin name for each species of plant has been by and large agreed upon across North America as well as the world. So we know that the plant called common chickweed in the United States and United Kingdom, *yin chai hu* in China, *hakobe* in Japan, and *la stellaire* in France is actually the same plant all over the world: *Stellaria media*.

To accurately identify a plant

SKIPPING THE MUSHROOM HUNT

Many people first think of mushrooms when they hear the word *foraging,* but we have chosen not to focus on mushrooms because they are not that accessible to many people across the country and because many edible mushrooms look almost identical to poisonous species. Instead we comment on only a handful of the most common and least likely to be confused. I make sure to consult with a mycologist (a mushroom scientist) who is prominent in our state's mycological association. Mushrooms are an important part of the ecology of the landscape and their associations with trees and the soil are critical, so it is important to harvest them in a limited and sustainable way.

family and species, I use the following checklist, which helps me gather necessary information:

- ❧ **Identify the broad category of the plant**—that is, tree, shrub, vine, herb, or grasslike plant.

- ❧ **Notice the place and conditions** where you find the plant, such as a sunny field, forest edge, or wet ground. Many of the plants in this book can be found in "disturbed" areas, ones that have been plowed or dug by humans, such as in a lawn, vegetable garden, or yard near the house.

- ❧ **Check the "growth habit,"** the way the plant grows—whether it is sprawling along the ground, for instance, or tall and upright. An important characteristic is whether the plant is usually found in a crowd or as single plants scattered here and there. Growth habit will be affected by the way the plant's root system grows. If a plant grows from underground rhizomes that spread to form large clonal (growing out from the same parent) stands, you are not likely to find it alone.

- ❧ **Note the time of year** when the plant is in a certain stage of growth. This book is arranged chronologically so that you can look for the plant or the right part of the plant (bud, young leaf, or flower) when the flavor is good. The photos and illustrations have been designed to capture the plant at the time when it is best for eating, which is not usually the case for most field guides.

- ❧ **Observe the key characteristics** of the plant. Don't worry about matching the exact color of a flower or size of a leaf to a photo or sketch. Due to seasonal weather, soil conditions, and just plain genetic variability, the same species will have individual differences, just as people have many colors of hair. For edible purposes, there are key identification characteristics to focus on that will be specific for each plant, which I've noted in each plant entry in the book. But the following are general areas to recognize, with the focus on identifying plants through their leaves, before they flower—the prime time for foraging.

Overall leaf formation: In early spring the leaves of many plants begin to grow all from one center point. This form is known as the basal rosette.

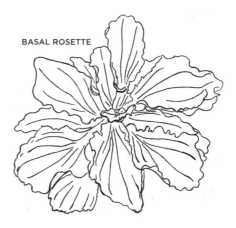

BASAL ROSETTE

OPPOSITE

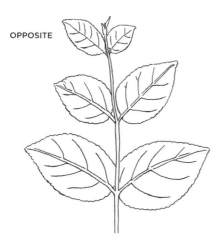

Leaf arrangement on stem or stalk: This may be "opposite," where the branches or leaves sit exactly opposite each other on the stem or trunk; "alternate," where the branches or leaves are staggered along the stem; or "whorled," where three or more leaves spiral around a stem.

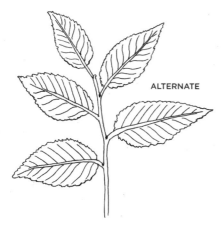

ALTERNATE

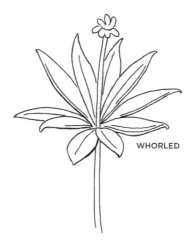

WHORLED

Leaf surface and texture: The leaf surface may have tiny hairs or be fuzzy; the veins running through the leaf may be straight and run to the edge or may be branched.

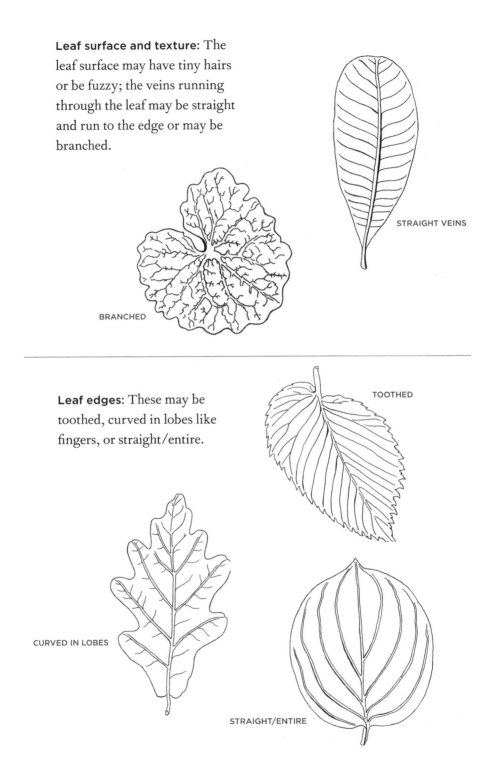

STRAIGHT VEINS

BRANCHED

Leaf edges: These may be toothed, curved in lobes like fingers, or straight/entire.

TOOTHED

CURVED IN LOBES

STRAIGHT/ENTIRE

General leaf shape: Overall the leaf may take a myriad of forms, only a few of which we note here as they relate to our featured plants: heart shaped, kidney shaped, ovate, and dissected, among others.

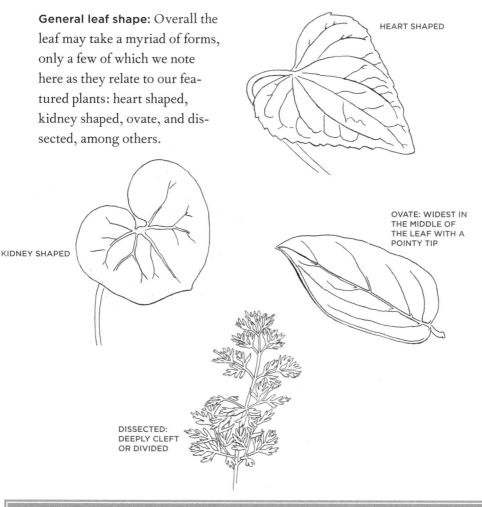

HEART SHAPED

OVATE: WIDEST IN THE MIDDLE OF THE LEAF WITH A POINTY TIP

KIDNEY SHAPED

DISSECTED: DEEPLY CLEFT OR DIVIDED

IN THE FIELD

I recommend the following gear when out foraging:

- Tall waterproof boots so you have no qualms about walking through any mud, poison ivy, or thorny bushes
- Kitchen scissors
- Kitchen garbage bags and/or one-gallon plastic bags with sliding zippers

- Heavy latex gloves (for nettles or aralia)
- Hat with a wide brim to keep off the sun as well as any small gnats or flies; in hunting season, wear a bright color

- Clothes with pockets
- Optional: camera, field guide, bottle of water

Stem: Turn the stem back and forth between your fingers to feel its shape; it may be round, triangular, flat, or—if you can feel four ridges—square.

Smell: Crush a leaf in your hand and smell the aroma. Once you have ruled out a number of plants based on structure and looks, the final check for many plants, such as mustards, mints, and garlicky edibles, is the aroma.

Flowers: In addition to the general color of any flowers, check how many petals a flower has. Note how the flowers are arranged, what the cluster looks like, and whether the flowers are directly joined to the stem. These include:

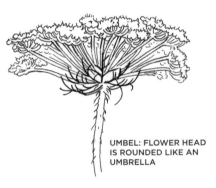

UMBEL: FLOWER HEAD IS ROUNDED LIKE AN UMBRELLA

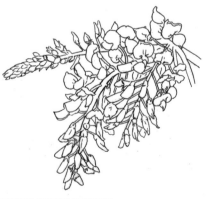

RACEME: OLDEST FLOWERS ARE AT THE BASE AND NEW FLOWERS ARE PRODUCED AS THE STEM GROWS. FLOWERS ARE ATTACHED TO THE STEM ON STALKS.

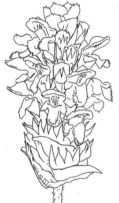

SPIKE: FLOWERS ARE ATTACHED RIGHT TO THE STEM

When I find a new plant (and every year there is something new), I go through my checklist and also take several photos, from close up as well as somewhat farther back, to note the general surroundings. I cross-check the plant on the Internet and in one or two field guides, comparing photos. If I am still not sure, I post a question to the botanist community on my website.

Once certain of the identification of the species, I check the sustainability status (see page 42) to determine whether I can responsibly pick it in the wild. I then make sure that I have permission from the landowner, if it is not on my property, and check that the surrounding area is sufficiently distant from chemical runoff, highway fumes, animal waste, and pesticides. Then, I take a sample and taste a small amount at home before I bring it to Eddy to try. This commonsense and risk-averse approach has worked for me for many years.

FROM FIELD TO KITCHEN

You'll find these helpful once you bring home your foraged finds: one or more colanders and strainers (of different sizes), a salad spinner, and a kitchen scale. To prepare plants for eating, carefully examine them and remove any diseased, brown, or stiff parts. Place the plants in a bowl of cold water and swirl them around gently, removing any stray twigs, other plants that may have inadvertently been mixed in, and little insect friends. Spin in a salad spinner to dry. Most wild greens and fresh flowers store well for up to a week in the refrigerator in a metal bin covered with plastic wrap over the top or in resealable plastic bags with a moistened paper towel inside. If you do this at the beginning of the week, soon after foraging, you have a refrigerator full of ingredients to use over the next week. Berries, seeds, and nuts on the other hand should be stored in open containers without moisture added. Store mushrooms in the refrigerator in a paper bag, never plastic.

Finally, note that while the recipes include measurements by both size and weight, particularly because of the variability in wild plants and their sizes, weight will be the most accurate. Also note that measurements called for in recipes are generally before chopping or cutting. Some plants, such as wisteria, pine, and rose branches or knotweed and nettle, may be particularly difficult to gauge in the field in terms of quantity because you will need to remove a fair amount of bulk after gathering them to get down to the usable ingredient. For these we give a ballpark amount to gather in order to ensure you will have enough to complete a recipe.

FORAGING SUSTAINABLY

Plants, like people, tend to hang out together and form communities. Some people love hot weather, sand, and sun. They form beach communities, they join clubs, they let friends and family know about good places, and then invite them to come on down. Same for plants. Some plants feel happy only when their feet are wet and mucky, whereas others are not too picky and can settle down anywhere. Some travel far and wide and some are homebodies; they need to stick around close to where they grew up. Scientists classify types of natural plant communities and what wild landscapes look like.

A number of plants like to grow where the latest "event" is happening, where the land has been disturbed, usually by humans, peeling back the skin of the earth so that the soil is exposed, plowing under trees and fields to make way for buildings, crops, or gardens. A botanist friend calls these plants "healing plants"; they are some of the first to rush to a disturbance and populate open ground, like a scab on a wound. You may have thought of them as weeds and nothing more, but I have grown to appreciate them as some of the easiest plants to find and, because of their way

of growing with abandon, some of the most sustainable to harvest.

You might think that because something is growing wild it is fine to harvest: If the plant found a way to grow on its own without any tending, surely it will continue to do so and will grow plentifully. But that is not always the case. As University of Delaware professor and chair of Entomology and Wildlife Ecology Doug Tallamy's fascinating research reveals, plants originating in a certain place have coevolved with certain insects and animals over the course of millions of years and do not readily switch to other insects or wildlife even in a couple hundred years, a mere fraction of that time. So plants that are part of the historical ecology of the landscape should be harvested on a limited basis or, instead, planted, because to deplete them will affect other species and life up the food chain. On the other end of the spectrum, some plants are not so joined to the underlying fabric of the local natural systems and may even threaten to push out others; these are prime foraging candidates.

Each plant in this book has been given a color code—Green, Yellow, or Red—to indicate its level on a sustainable foraging scale, from go (Green) to stop (Red).

- **Green:** Naturalized and invasive plants; safe to forage without limit. These plants came mostly from Europe or Asia and were brought over as familiar foods or on the boots of the first European settlers and then later on ships and goods in trade with Asia. Many of these plants, such as dandelion, Queen Anne's lace, chicory, plantain, and chickweed, have escaped from gardens or otherwise "naturalized" and now grow wild along fields and roadsides. Invasive plants (sometimes called "noxious" weeds) have found living too easy because their new home lacks the predators and natural controls to keep them in check. Others exude substances that kill and suppress the growth of their neighbors. These plants, such as knotweed, multiflora rose, Asian honeysuckle, and garlic mustard, replicate and spread aggressively, causing ecological imbalances in their newfound habitat. In fact, governments often spend many dollars on their removal. Needless to say, care must be taken not to spread the seeds of these plants when foraging.

- **Yellow:** Generalist native plants; harvest on a limited basis. Native plants have coevolved with the local landscape and its natural ecological systems. Ecologists further distinguish these plants as "generalists" or "specialists" (see Red, below). Generalists don't sweat the small stuff, such as whether the soil is acidic, or require a certain type of rock outcropping to bloom; they are more easygoing about where and with whom they choose to grow. They adapt to disturbance and will generally grow back, provided they are not dug up by the roots. A good rule of thumb is to limit your picking to 20 percent of what you find, leaving the rest for the wildlife.

- **Red:** Specialist and conservative native plants; plant and pick only from your garden. Specialist plants are fussier about where they live than generalist ones and they don't take well to change. They may require special conditions and interactions with underground fungi, tree roots, or leaves on a damp forest floor to grow. If their patch of earth is plowed under or otherwise disturbed, they may take many years to regrow, if they do at all. Many, but not all, rare, endangered, and extinct plants are specialists, but—even if not yet designated by a conservation organization as a species of concern that is declining and currently in need of conservation—specialist native plants should not be harvested in the wild because of the high risk that they may not grow back. The tasty ones that we have included in this book are available in specialty nurseries and online.

A WILD KITCHEN GARDEN

Wild food grows all around us, in ordinary places—jumping out of our lawns, a vacant lot or vegetable garden, on the edges of forests and farm fields. Take a closer look at some plants you have always seen hanging around but never thought twice about. Chances are great that one or more of them is in this cookbook.

If you do not have an area around you to forage, you can create one in a 3 × 6-foot space. Almost any plot, from a small urban lot to a suburban lawn to a large open field, can be made into a low-labor wild space prime for foraging plants such as anise hyssop, stinging nettle, purslane, lambsquar-

ters, bee balm, and lavender bergamot. Just follow these guidelines:

- Start clean: Stop applying chemicals and/or spraying the area that you want to turn wild (including areas around it where water runs down into the wild patch). If you live next to a busy street or have an old foundation, you may want to have the soil tested for lead or other contaminants, as you would for a vegetable garden. If in doubt, you can also opt for a raised garden bed.

- But don't tidy up too much: Wild plants, like many youngsters, will not thrive in an overorganized, sterile environment. So leave some "debris," including leaf litter and old organic matter leftover from the year, to replenish the soil and encourage growth.

- Don't mow an area of lawn in the spring unless your grass grows so high as to crowd out other species. I found a season's worth of foraged foods simply by not mowing until after the dandelions bloomed. And I could see lots of great things in other people's lawns but since they had already been mowed down to two inches in March, there wasn't enough to eat. If good stuff comes up that you like, let it go to seed and mark that area for next spring.

❧ In an organic vegetable garden or garden bed, skip the heavy layers of mulch and start paying attention to your weeds. You can extend your edible growing season through frost and beyond by eating the wild greens that spring up, untended. By the time we were just ready to enjoy fresh peas from our garden, we had already been eating wild plants for four months. Growing wild plants side by side with vegetables seems to increase their pest resistance and certainly increases the richness of the soil.

❧ Plant foraging level—Red plants within "kitchen garden" distance from your house. The good news is, since they are native and grow wild naturally in this country, you should not have to prop them up or force-feed them to survive. You also won't have to amend the soil since native plants generally like poorer soils. The first season, water them to make sure they settle in, and check that they are in the right area for sun or shade, wet or dry. Then let them be and harvest what they bear for your table.

If you live in a city and don't have a small garden or compost pile, look into sharing an urban community garden plot. Or contact a nearby organic or community-supported agriculture (CSA) farm and volunteer to help weed. Get in touch with your local park or conservation group to inquire about participating in an invasive plant foraging hike. You can also "forage" the stands at farmer's markets for plants such as lambsquarters, nettles, and purslane.

Weeds . . . are the truer crop which the earth more willingly bears.
—Henry David Thoreau

EARLY SPRING

It's almost spring. There is something about the quality of the light that begins to change. Chilly nights and cool mornings give way to a kind of midday glow when I can feel the warmth of the sun on my face. I am impatient, waiting for the snow to clear and for the first tiny green shoots to emerge from the earth.

When everything looks so brown and gray, it is an act of faith to believe that the land will soon turn green again. For me, every spring, year after year, a little miracle happens when the green plants begin to stretch their arms out of the seemingly dead ground. Sometimes I can find the white sprouts underneath last year's leaves. Easy to name when flowering or three feet high, they make me guess at who they are under their early disguise.

Wild plants emerge much earlier than farm crops. Frost-hardy wild garlic, chickweed, cardamine, henbit, and garlic mustard awaken while the soil is still stiff and crackly, months before the first corn or beans can be planted or even before you see the tree leaves. Many cultures have a tradition of celebrating early spring greens for their taste, for health, and for their symbolic rejuvenation: the Japanese *nanakusa* celebration of the seven wild herbs of spring; the Korean *namul* tradition, where each spring mothers and daughters gather wild herbs from mountains and fields; the European taste for wild herbal liquors known as bitters; and the Italian Genovese seven-wild-herb mixture known as *preboggion* used in risotto and ravioli. For many wild plants, spring is when their shoots and leaves are at their culinary best, tender and full of sweet flavor, turning bitter or tough at maturity.

When Eddy thinks of the taste of spring, he conjures wild greens, fresh with a little bite. For many spring greens, their fanciful and sometimes strange-sounding names belie a treasure trove of flavors and textures: bitter, sweet, sour, oniony, garlicky, crunchy, juicy, tender, and stiff, found in a number of forms, from shoots and creeping herbs to buds and delicate flowers.

WILD GARLIC *Allium vineale* (see photographs pages 22 and 26)

Foraging level: Green **Form:** Herb (shoots, underground bulbs, and aerial bulblets) **Found in:** Lawns, edges of forests and fields throughout most of the United States and Canada (excluding the Rocky Mountain states and the Southwest).	**Growth habit:** Upright, spreading in clumps, from a few inches to 1 to 2 feet high as shoots. **Key characteristics:** Looks similar to chives but more delicate, with round (not flat) hollow stems; garlicky aroma when torn.	**Harvest tips:** Choose thinner shoots and pull off handfuls at the base or snip with scissors. Thicker shoots can be used in stews and soups.

In the late winter and early spring, when the farmer's markets are shuttered and the fields and forests are brown, I am out scouting for the green shoots of wild garlic. When they grow to more than a couple of inches high I begin to bring them in bagfuls to Eddy. From the very beginning, wild garlic has been one of his favorites for its not-too-sharp flavor, which is subtle and quite a unique blend of chive and garlic.

FORAGER'S JOURNAL

This past November, the second-grade Brownie troop at Princeton Day School asked me to lead them on a foraging hike to earn their next nature badge. The girls are naturals in the field, and they immediately recognize wild garlic shoots, which reappear on cold autumn days. "Onion grass!" they shout, pulling the greens out in handfuls, eating them on the spot, and breathing in deeply the garlicky aroma.

Scrambled Eggs with Wild Garlic Greens

This is Eddy's take on bagels, lox, and cream cheese for foragers. The garlicky taste balances the salmon, along with the creaminess of the egg and a touch of sour cream. Good for a hearty brunch on a rainy cold day. ❧ **Serves 4**

1 tablespoon unsalted butter
8 large eggs, lightly beaten
4 ounces sliced smoked salmon, cut into strips
2 tablespoons sour cream
½ ounce (¼ cup) finely chopped wild garlic greens
2 English muffins or bagels, split in half and toasted
Salt and freshly ground black pepper

In a medium skillet, melt the butter over medium heat and pour in the eggs. Stir continuously with a wooden spoon for about 3 minutes, or until they hold very soft moist curds. Remove from the heat and stir in the salmon, sour cream, and wild garlic greens. Spoon equal portions onto the muffin halves. Sprinkle with salt and pepper.

Wild Garlic Greens and Potato Pancakes

These crispy pancakes, with the extra zing of wild garlic, are a great brunch addition on chilly mornings or an accompaniment to a braised meat supper. ✨ **Serves 4 to 6**

> 3 medium Yukon gold potatoes (about 1 pound)
> 2 large eggs
> 3 tablespoons all-purpose flour
> ¼ cup plus 2 tablespoons finely chopped wild garlic greens
> 1 small white onion, finely chopped
> 3 tablespoons grapeseed or canola oil, plus more as needed
> Salt and freshly ground black pepper

1. Peel the potatoes and shred them on the medium holes of a box grater. Press excess water out of the potatoes by hand.

2. In a medium bowl, beat the eggs, then mix in the flour, wild garlic greens, onion, and potato.

3. In a large skillet, heat the oil over medium heat. Drop a large dollop (about ¼ cup) of the potato mixture into the pan. Lightly press it down with the back of a spatula so that it flattens like a pancake, 3 to 4 inches across and ¼ to ½ inch thick. Drop in several more, depending on the size of your skillet. When golden brown on one side, 2 to 3 minutes, flip the pancakes and brown the other side, about 2 minutes. Season with salt and pepper.

4. Remove and pat dry with paper towels. Repeat, adding more oil to the pan as necessary. Serve hot.

Pickled Wild Garlic Bulbs

When you notice the garlic shoots growing thick and they begin to taste sharp, you can lightly dig up the small plump bulbs with a small trowel. For dinner at home, we eat these as a condiment with beef stew. ❧ **Makes 1 pint**

> **Handful of wild garlic bulbs (10 to 20), greens attached**
> **1 cup distilled or rice vinegar**
> **3 tablespoons sugar**
> **Pinch of red pepper flakes**

In a small pot, bring the wild garlic bulbs, vinegar, sugar, and red pepper flakes to a boil. Immediately reduce the heat to low and simmer for 5 minutes. Remove from the heat and let cool. Refrigerate for up to a few weeks.

LESSER CELANDINE *Ranunculus ficaria*
Foraging level: Green

This invasive herbaceous plant grows on shady moist ground and creek beds in the northeast, central, and northwestern United States and Canada. The same Eurasian fig buttercup is also the French *le ficaire.* The rosettes of tender heart-shaped, bluntly toothed, 1- to 2-inch leaves emerge extremely early in the spring. They bloom with star-bright yellow flowers and the greens disappear soon after the leaves unfurl in the forest. (Do not mistake these with marsh marigold, which has larger leaves and is foraging level red.) The tubers are tasty when fried in a beer batter, although small and tedious to wash and separate for cooking. The leaves need to be consumed raw and young, before flowering, or they can become quite acrid. If you have a ready, overabundant supply, toss the leaves as a salad with a sweet citrus dressing.

HENBIT *Lamium amplexicaule* (SEE PHOTOGRAPH PAGE 21)
and DEADNETTLE *Lamium purpureum* (SEE PHOTOGRAPH PAGE 19)

Foraging level: Green

Form: Herb (leaves, flowers, young stems)

Found in: Sunny disturbed open ground, lawns, garden beds, and field edges throughout the United States and Canada.

Growth habit: Sprawling and spreading, from 1 inch to 1 foot high.

Key characteristics: Both deadnettle and henbit are originally from Eurasia and belong to the larger mint family. They have square stems, opposite leaves, and reddish-purple to purple flowers. The distinctions between the two are subtle and can be best described by looking at the top of the plant as if it were a hat. In Japan, the white-flowered deadnettle is called *odoriko-so,* dancing lady's hat, because the top has a reddish or purple tinge to it and the flowers stick out of the top in a carefree way. The henbit, though, wears more of a shaggy wig on her top, without the purple tinge, and the leaves are much more lobed and jaggedly round. The flowers stick up quirkily. The henbit leaves are scrawny but thick and ruffled as compared with the deadnettle.

Harvest tips: Pull out handfuls or cut with scissors from the time of early leaves through flowering. Use the top 3 to 5 inches of fresh growth and discard the rest.

Henbit and deadnettle are early signs of green, right out there growing through the frost. I didn't know they were edible until I learned that people in Asia and France feast on them in the spring. There are lots all over my backyard, so I pull out a bagful and bring some in to Eddy . . . he frowns at the unfamiliar names. "Deadnettle? Tama, our diners will not like to see a menu with the word *dead* on it. And *henbit,* it is one word?" I tell him it sounds strange but it is named so because chickens like to eat it. "Hmm . . . okay," he says, but once he tastes it: "Oh, nice! Fresh, subtle, herbal, hints of celery." The henbit tastes slightly nutty, whereas the deadnettle has a hint of sour.

Wild Herb Ravioli

You can taste wild spring in this dish: the fusion of herbal flavors of the deadnettle and its slight sourness, the fresh mild chickweed, and the bite of the wild garlic. If you don't feel like making homemade pasta, use a 16-ounce package of egg roll wrappers. ❧ **Serves 6**

WILD HERB FILLING
3 tablespoons unsalted butter, plus more for serving
1½ ounces (2 cups firmly packed) chickweed (see page 64)
   or spinach, stiff stems removed
1 ounce (1½ cups firmly packed) deadnettle or henbit tops,
   including flowers
1 ounce (¾ cup) wild garlic greens or chives, snipped
   into ½- to 1-inch lengths
Salt and freshly ground black pepper
2 ounces (¼ cup) ricotta cheese
½ cup freshly grated Parmesan cheese, plus more for serving

PASTA DOUGH
1 cup 00 or all-purpose flour, plus more for dusting
2 large eggs
1 tablespoon plus 1½ teaspoons olive oil
¼ teaspoon salt

1. Make the filling: In a medium skillet, melt 1 tablespoon of the butter and add the chickweed, deadnettle, and wild garlic greens. Cook for about 2 minutes over medium heat, or until bright green and soft.

2. Transfer the cooked herb mixture to a food processor and chop for less than a minute. Season with a pinch each of salt and pepper. With a spoon, transfer to a medium bowl and mix in the ricotta cheese and Parmesan. Set aside to cool.

3. Make the dough: In a medium bowl, using your hands, mix together the flour, one of the eggs, the yolk of the remaining egg (reserve the white), 1½ teaspoons of the oil, and the salt. Transfer to a floured work surface and knead the dough for 4 to 5 minutes, or until smooth and elastic. Divide in half, wrap in plastic, and let rest in the refrigerator (preferably overnight but for at least 30 minutes).

4. Roll out the dough into two very thin sheets, using either a rolling pin or a pasta machine at one notch from the thinnest setting. Drop teaspoonfuls of filling an inch apart over one sheet of the dough. Dip your finger in water or use the remaining egg white and trace a circle around each teaspoon of filling. Then place the other sheet of dough on top, making sure to force out any air, and press to seal. Using a 2-inch ring cutter, ravioli cutter, inverted glass, or a knife, cut out each ravioli. Check each one to make sure it is sealed. The ravioli can be made hours ahead of time, covered, and refrigerated, or frozen on a baking sheet and then stored in a zipper-top freezer bag.

5. To cook the pasta, bring a large pot of salted water to a boil and add the remaining 1 tablespoon olive oil. Cook the ravioli in batches for 3 to 5 minutes, or until the pasta is translucent and you can see the herbs inside. Drain well. Serve topped with the remaining 2 tablespoons butter and a sprinkling of Parmesan.

FORAGER'S JOURNAL

The wild herb ravioli garnished with black trumpet mushrooms, cardamine, and Spanish ham were flying out of the restaurant kitchen! How exciting to see the plants go from their country duds to star attire in the city. But their popularity meant I had to bring in enough to make more than two hundred "covers" (orders) a week. My kitchen garbage bags were breaking under the weight, and I had to leave the subway during rush hour as I took up enough space for four people, jostling and irritating everyone around me with my amoeba-like spreading bags. The final straw was when I tried to put everything in one of those collapsible metal carts people use to wheel their groceries home. The wheels didn't turn well and the cart fell apart trying to get through the entrance doors to the PATH commuter train, wheels spinning left and right. The security guards felt sorry for me on that rainy morning and kindly assisted me and my bags into a taxi. Of course, wouldn't you know, once my New Jersey taxi reached New York City, we were stopped by the police, who insisted on looking in the bags and sniffing around at the plants. I don't think they recognized any of the smells they were looking for, and they eventually let me continue on to the restaurant. It was right about then that I gave up on the subway and started driving into the city. Eddy arrives hours early and helps me carry the bags out of the trunk of the car. While he is inspecting and washing everything in the kitchen, we can talk about the plants.

Deadnettle Velouté

This velvety smooth soup is based on Arborio rice, which gives a creamy yet light (and dairy-free) consistency. It warms you up on those early spring nights with the chill still in the air, and is filling enough for a supper before a fire or in the den. The taste and texture are very mild, so serve with crusty bread, some cheese, or charcuterie on the side.

❧ **Serves 6**

> 2 ounces (3 cups firmly packed) deadnettle tops, including flowers
> 1 quart plus ¼ cup low-sodium chicken stock or broth
> ⅔ cup Arborio rice, rinsed
> Salt
> 1 tablespoon fresh lemon juice

1. Have ready a large bowl of ice water. In a large pot over high heat, bring salted water to a boil. Add the deadnettle and cook for 2 to 3 minutes, or until tender.

2. Drain the deadnettle and transfer to the ice water to cool. This step is important because it seals in the lovely spring green color of the leaves and also keeps them from overcooking. Drain well, squeezing out excess water. Puree the deadnettle in a food processor with ¼ cup of the chicken stock. Spoon into a bowl.

3. In a large pot, combine the rice, remaining quart of chicken stock, and 2 cups water. Bring to a simmer over low heat and cook for about 30 minutes, or until the rice is completely tender. In batches, ladle the rice and broth into a blender or food processor. Blend well for a full minute, or until the mixture becomes frothy and smooth. (You should see a number of tiny bubbles on the surface like foam.)

4. Strain each batch back into the large pot through a fine strainer to be sure it is silky and not lumpy. Stir the deadnettle puree into the rice broth. Season with salt and add the lemon juice to bring out the flavor. Serve warm.

Eddy and I still can't agree on what to call this recipe. I say many people in the United States may not know that a velouté is a thick soup, not a chowder or a stew.

"So call it 'soup,'" he says.

"But it is so much more than just a soup," I protest. "How about 'bisque'?"

"No, no, Tama. Bisque must be for the shellfish type."

There are so many words in French for different kinds of soups but not enough in English!

CORN SPEEDWELL *Veronica arvensis*

Foraging level: Green

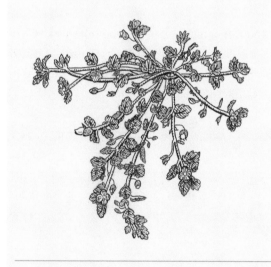

A common low-growing herbaceous weed found in farm fields, lawns, garden beds, and sunny open disturbed areas throughout the United States and Canada (excluding North Dakota), the corn speedwell belongs to the *Veronica* tribe. This *Veronica* has opposite, roundish, small-toothed leaves and its blooms are pretty, tiny 1/4-inch blue stalkless flowers. The taste is mild although not particularly distinctive. Eddy made a yogurt dressing for a corn speedwell salad with rhubarb. In the restaurant they serve it as a fresh raw salad as well as a garnish for fish dishes. Harvest when young or in bloom and use only the top few inches, not the rambling stems.

Sautéed Henbit with Fava Beans and Cipollini Onions

This recipe gives the henbit a chance to show off her personal style. The ruffly texture of the leaves and their nutty taste balance the smoothness of the fava beans and cipollini. This makes a nice side dish for a spring dinner with lamb seasoned with Garlic Mustard Oil (page 73) and served with mashed potatoes. ❧ **Serves 4**

6 ounces shelled fava beans (about 3 pounds before shelling)
   or green peas
4 tablespoons (½ stick) unsalted butter
6 medium cipollini, sliced
4 ounces (5 to 6 cups) henbit tops, including flowers
1 cup low-sodium chicken stock or broth
Salt and freshly ground black pepper

1. Have ready a large bowl of ice water. In a medium pot, bring salted water to a boil. Add the fava beans and cook for about 10 seconds, then drain the beans and transfer to the ice water to cool. Drain the beans and then remove the outer skin of each bean, popping the favas out of their skins.

2. Melt the butter in a large skillet over medium heat. (It is important to use a pan with a large cooking surface so the liquid will reduce quickly.) Add the onions and cook for 2 minutes, or until softened. Add the fava beans, henbit, and chicken stock and continue to cook, stirring, for about 4 minutes, or until the liquid has reduced to a shiny glaze but has not completely evaporated. Season with salt and pepper and serve.

Chicken Salad with Henbit and Avocado

In this dish, the frilly texture of raw henbit balances the smooth and creamy avocado; jalapeño and salty capers add a little kick. This is a mosaic of spring colors: light green, dark green, and flecks of purple.

🍃 **Serves 4**

2 Hass avocados, peeled and pitted
2 cooked boneless skinless chicken breast halves, shredded
2 ounces (1½ cups) henbit tops, preferably with purple flowers
1 jalapeño, stemmed, seeded, and finely chopped
2 tablespoons drained brined small capers
3 tablespoons fresh lime juice
½ cup extra-virgin olive oil, plus more for drizzling
Salt and freshly ground black pepper

1. Dice one of the avocados and put it in a large bowl. Add the chicken, henbit, jalapeño, and capers.

2. In a food processor or blender, puree the remaining avocado with the lime juice while pouring in the olive oil in a constant stream for 1 to 2 minutes, or until the dressing becomes smooth and creamy. Season with salt and pepper.

3. Spoon the dressing over the salad and toss, making sure to coat the henbit.

FRAGRANT BEDSTRAW *Galium triflorum*

(SEE PHOTOGRAPH PAGE 20)

Foraging level: Yellow

Form: Herb (young tops with leaves and stem)

Found in: Sunny or partly shaded disturbed ground, vegetable gardens, garden beds, and yards; grows throughout the United States.

Growth habit: Sprawling, low growing, tucked here and there in groups.

Key characteristics: Six leaves in a whorl attach to a smooth stem, and leaves are tipped with bristles. Other species in the *Galium* clan are also edible and are characterized by small whorls of four to six leaves and prickly hooks, giving them the nickname the "cleaver," as they stick or cleave to you.

Harvest tips: Pinch or cut off the top 3 to 6 inches of each sprig.

Eddy is charmed by the beautiful and intricate architectural whorled structures of these small herbs, twirling them between his fingers. The taste when very young is fresh but not grassy, with a little jolt of acidity that goes well with fish. Eddy is always talking to me about the importance of acidity, which gives a dish some structure to bring out hidden flavors and character.

FORAGER'S JOURNAL

"Bedstraw" was another common name that Eddy cringed at putting on the menu, preferring "Galium" instead!

Galium Potato Chips

These chips taste and look exquisite. You can see the beautiful herb inside the actual chip, captured between the thin potato slices like a flower pressed between book pages. ❧ **Makes 8 large chips**

    1 large Idaho potato
    2 medium egg yolks, lightly beaten
    8 sprigs of galium, only the top 3 inches
    Handful of all-purpose flour
    Vegetable oil
    Salt

1. Peel and very thinly slice the potato into 16 slices, preferably using a mandoline. Save 1 scrap of potato for testing the oil later. Brush 1 side of 1 potato slice with egg yolk. Arrange 1 galium sprig in the middle. Set another potato slice on top like a sandwich and press the slices firmly together with your fingers. Make 8 chip sandwiches this way. Dip the double-layer chips lightly in flour, tapping off the excess.

2. Heat 1 inch of oil in a frying pan to about 350°F. The test piece of potato should sizzle when dropped in the oil. Fry the potato chips a couple at a time, turning them over, until the edges get crispy, about 2 minutes. Remove from the oil, transfer to a paper towel–lined plate and pat dry with another paper towel to remove any excess oil. While the chips are still warm, push down any bubbly areas so you can see the outline of the herb through the translucent potato. Season with salt and serve hot.

CHICKWEED *Stellaria media* (SEE PHOTOGRAPH PAGE 18)

Foraging level: Green

Form: Herb (leaves, young stems, and white flowers)

Found in: Sunny open disturbed ground, farm fields, vegetable gardens, garden beds, lawns, and open forest paths throughout the United States and Canada as well as much of the temperate world.

Growth habit: Sprawling, low growing.

Key characteristics: Soft stems bear rounded opposite leaves with pointy tips. Check that the underside of the leaf is not spotted and that there is no milky sap. The flower is tiny white, not orange.

Harvest tips: Choose fresh lush green plants and pull out in clumps. Pluck off the tender tips—usually 3 to 5 inches long. Leaves soon turn yellow and wilt, so it is usually best to pick within a few days of eating. Remove any brown or tough stalks.

When I mention chickweed to my neighboring farmer, he makes an exasperated face about this tiresome weed that he can't seem to get rid of, like a salesperson who always calls at the door and hangs around. But chickweed does have something good to sell it, appearing early in the spring when not much is green yet. Chickweed is celebrated as one of Japan's seven wild herbs of spring, cooked in a warm rice porridge. When chickweed is raw it can taste grassy; with cooking it becomes milder and more like tender spinach. Eddy favors the chickweed that grows alongside open forest paths among the moist leaf litter, smelling like fresh microgreens.

Chickweed with Sesame and Soy Sauce

This easy-peasy side dish was inspired by the classic soy-sesame combination in Asian home-style cooking. Serve with hot steamed rice and roast pork or grilled fish. ❧ **Serves 4 as a small side dish**

¼ **cup sesame seeds**
1 tablespoon toasted sesame oil
1 small onion, finely chopped
2 garlic cloves, minced
4 ounces (5 cups) tender chickweed greens
1 tablespoon light soy sauce or tamari
1 teaspoon sugar
Pinch of red pepper flakes
Pinch of salt

1. In a small pan (cast iron is great), spread out the sesame seeds and toast over medium-low heat for 2 minutes, or until about half of them pop and turn a light golden brown. Transfer to a small bowl and set aside.

2. In a medium skillet, heat the sesame oil, onion, and garlic for about 2 minutes, or until soft. Add the chickweed and cook for 3 minutes, or until soft. Remove from the heat.

3. Mix in the soy sauce, sugar, red pepper flakes, salt, and sesame seeds. Serve warm or at room temperature.

Chickweed Crostini

Chickweed and other wild greens make a fresh-tasting topper for toast, bruschetta, or an English muffin. Eddy loves this crostini appetizer with tangy Gorgonzola and walnuts for both spring and fall.

 Serves 4

1 tablespoon plus 2 teaspoons olive oil
6 ounces (about ½ loaf) country bread, baguette, or
    other crusty bread, sliced 1 inch thick
1 small white onion, chopped
1 ounce (1¼ cups) tender chickweed greens or other wild green
    such as galium or cress, plus more for serving
1½ ounces Gorgonzola or other tangy blue cheese
2 tablespoons heavy cream
1 tablespoon chopped walnuts

1. In a large skillet, heat 2 teaspoons of the olive oil over medium-high heat; add the bread, pressing down on the slices. Toast each side until lightly browned.

2. In a medium skillet, heat the remaining 1 tablespoon olive oil over medium heat. Add the onion and cook for 2 minutes, or until softened. Add the chickweed and cook for a few minutes, or until tender and bright green.

3. Meanwhile, in a small pot, melt the Gorgonzola and cream over low heat.

4. Spoon equal portions of the chickweed on top of each bread slice and drizzle with the cheese sauce. Sprinkle with walnuts and a few raw sprigs of chickweed and serve.

CARDAMINE or HAIRY BITTER CRESS

Cardamine hirsuta (SEE PHOTOGRAPH PAGE 17)

Foraging level: Green

Form: Herb (leaves, flowers)

Found in: Moist disturbed areas, lawns, and garden beds throughout most of the United States and Canada (excluding the Plains states).

Growth habit: Small, sprawling, low growing, becoming more upright as it flowers.

Key characteristics: Cardamine starts as a swirling green pinwheel rosette; each leaflet has its own stem. As the plant grows, tiny white flowers stick up straight from the center perched like a swan's head on a long neck, but not taller than 6 to 8 inches.

Harvest tips: Choose plants with lush green leaves in order to have enough volume for these recipes. The entire plant pulls out with minimal effort. Remove and discard the basal rosette center where all the leaves join and also any stiff stems that may emerge after flowering.

Through the chilly winds and frosts of early spring, *Cardamine hirsuta* is happy and humming. Her leaves are tender and have a light peppery zing. Eddy often asks me about her. The kitchen staff must wonder what old friend of his has such an interesting name as they overhear him talking to me on the phone. "How is cardamine? Have you seen cardamine?" Although sometimes called "hairy bitter cress," we just call her cardamine, as she tastes neither bitter nor hairy and is not related to the watercress found in streams.

NARROWLEAF BITTERCRESS *cardamine impatiens*

Foraging level: Green

Cardamine impatiens, commonly known as narrowleaf bittercress, another European import, has a later season and so becomes a great substitute when the *hirsuta* starts going to seed. You will find this invasive in open or disturbed woodlands, especially along trails. The alternate leaves are more lobed than those of hirsute. The plant starts as a low basal rosette and long low leaflets that become more long and pointy as the plant matures to about 2 feet high. The stem is smooth and rigid, and where the leaf base meets the stem, you can see little downward pointing green appendages. Do not substitute other cardamines as many are foraging level Red.

Cardamine Cress and Hearty Pork Rib Soup

When my husband has the flu and wants Chinese comfort food, my mother-in-law makes a pork, ginger, and cress soup. Eddy adds plum to give a little sweetness and to contrast with the slight peppery zing of the wild cardamine. After all, plums and pork are a favorite pairing in French cooking, and dried plums are a Chinese food staple. On a cold rainy spring afternoon, this soothing soup lingers like a warm smile in our bellies. ❧ Serves 6

2 quarts low-sodium chicken stock or broth, or water
1 pound baby back pork ribs, split into sections
4 medium carrots, sliced about ½ inch thick
2 celery stalks, sliced about ½ inch thick
4 ounces pitted dried plums (about 3 large), cut into 1-inch chunks
2 bunches scallions (about 16), whites and the lower 4 inches of green, chopped
5 ounces (4 cups loosely packed) cardamine, basal rosette centers and stiff parts removed
2 generous pinches of red pepper flakes
Salt

1. In a large deep pot, bring the chicken stock and 2 cups water to a boil over high heat. Add the ribs, reduce the heat to medium, and cook for 20 minutes, or until the meat is tender. Skim off the foam that accumulates on the surface of the liquid so that the broth remains relatively clear.

2. Add the carrots and celery. Cover and let the soup simmer for 45 minutes.

3. Add the dried plums and cook for another 15 minutes. Stir in the scallions, cardamine, and red pepper flakes and season with salt. Reduce the heat to low and cook, covered, for about 15 minutes, or until the cardamine is soft and the plums look tender and melty. Serve hot.

Cardamine Cress with Fennel and Orange Vinaigrette

With this salad, you get everything in one bite: lively, peppery *Cardamine hirsuta*; sweet orange; and crunchy, licorice-y fennel. ❧ **Serves 4**

1 large fennel bulb
1 cup extra-virgin olive oil
1 tablespoon fennel seeds
1 star anise
2 pinches of red pepper flakes
Salt
3 medium oranges or tangerines
10 strands saffron (optional)
4 ounces (3 cups loosely packed) cardamine, basal rosette centers
    and stiff parts removed

1. Trim the fennel stalks and bottom. Halve the bulb and remove the core. Cut the fennel into 2-inch chunks. (Note: Don't waste the core or "heart." It can be thinly shaved and adds a magical crunch to the top of this salad.)

2. In a small pot, combine the fennel chunks, olive oil, fennel seeds, star anise, and red pepper flakes and season with salt. Cook over low heat for about 15 minutes, or until the fennel is tender. Remove the fennel and pat dry. Save ½ cup (or more to taste) of the spice-infused oil for the dressing.

3. Using a paring knife, peel the oranges, removing all of the pith and a sliver of the fruit all around. Cut between the orange membranes, releasing the segments into a medium bowl. Squeeze the membranes, reserving the juice. Measure ¼ cup juice and pour it into another medium bowl. Whisk in the infused olive oil to taste, the saffron, if using, and a pinch or two of salt.

4. Divide the cardamine, fennel, and orange segments among individual serving bowls and spoon the dressing over each salad.

Smoked Salmon with Cardamine Cress Mousseline and Lemon Sauce

The mousseline, spiked with barely cooked wild cress, tastes fresh, green, and peppery. The lemon yellow of the sauce, the orange of the salmon, and the green of the cardamine also make a pretty presentation to serve for guests. The mousseline and lemon sauce can be made ahead of time separately, then pulled together when ready to serve. Our testers loved this recipe so much that they started foraging their neighbors' backyards for more cardamine, and once they looked for it, they soon realized it was all over the place. ⌣ **Serves 4**

> 5 ounces (4 cups loosely packed) cardamine, basal rosette centers
>   and stiff parts removed, plus more for serving
> 1/3 cup heavy cream
> 1 tablespoon Dijon mustard
> 1/3 cup extra-virgin olive oil
> Grated zest of 1/2 lemon
> 1/4 cup fresh lemon juice
> Freshly ground black pepper
> 16 medium slices smoked salmon

1. Have ready a large bowl of ice water. In a medium pot, bring salted water to a boil. Add the cardamine and cook for less than 1 minute, or until bright green. Drain the cardamine and transfer to the ice water to cool. Drain well. Puree in a food processor, adding a teaspoon of water if needed.

2. In an electric mixer, whip the cream to stiff peaks. Gently whisk in the cardamine puree and mustard.

3. Whisk together the olive oil, lemon zest, and juice in a bowl. Season with pepper.

4. To serve, arrange the salmon slices on plates and top with a dollop of mousseline and a few spoons of lemon sauce. Generously garnish with raw sprigs of cardamine.

Fresh Oysters with Cardamine Cress Shallot Puree

The peppery taste and tender texture of the cardamine dances with the sea flavors of oysters in this recipe, which features a wild alternative to the usual mignonette sauce. ❦ **Serves 4 to 6**

> 20 raw oysters, such as kushi or kumamoto
> 2½ cups (3 ounces) cardamine, basal rosette centers and stiff parts removed
> ⅓ cup red wine vinegar
> 1 small shallot, finely chopped
> 1 tablespoon freshly ground black pepper

1. Brush the oysters under cold running water to remove any excess sand. Carefully open the shells with an oyster knife, prying at one edge. Set the open oysters on their half shells on a platter of crushed ice.

2. Bring a medium pot of salted water to a boil and add the cardamine. Cook for less than 1 minute, or until it turns bright green. Transfer to a bowl of ice water to cool. Drain well and transfer to a food processor. Process to a very fine puree. You should have about ⅓ cup puree.

3. In a small bowl, mix together the cardamine puree, vinegar, shallot, and pepper. Spoon the sauce liberally onto the oysters and slurp!

GARLIC MUSTARD *Alliaria petiolata* (SEE PHOTOGRAPH PAGE 20)

Foraging level: Green

Form: Herb (leaves, flowers)

Found in: Forests, forest edges, and shady roadsides in much of the United States and Canada (excluding the Southwest, Texas, and Florida).

Growth habit: Large invasive stands; starts as a basal rosette, often with large yellowing leaves left over from the previous winter, then grows upright later in the season to 1 to 3 feet tall.

Key characteristics: In early spring, under the bare trees and winter's leftover brown leaves, you can find garlic mustard rosettes and their crinkly heart-shaped leaves, which form a small U shape where the leaf joins the purplish stem. This rosette will grow new light green leaves and shoot up suddenly like an adolescent; small white flowers will bloom. Crush a leaf for a garlicky aroma.

Harvest tips: Grasp the part of the plant where the stem meets the roots and pluck the entire plant out of the ground. It will come out easily. Pick off the fresh, tender leaves.

Each year, garlic mustard can stealthily spread several thousand seeds, which may remain dormant for more than five years, waiting for the right conditions to sprout. When the seeds do begin to grow, garlic mustard can become a downright bully, taking over the plant neighborhood by releasing chemicals in the soil that interfere with the fungi—tree root associations and tree growth. The species also works a double shift, growing not only in the spring but also in the fall, when many plants have gone to sleep.

Eddy finds the flavor easy to like, better when raw, with a mild garlicky taste. The new-growth leaves, whether toward the center of the rosette or at the top of the plant, are more tender and tastier than the larger yellowing leaves. Freely substitute garlic mustard for basil in your favorite pesto recipe, but since there is ever so much garlic mustard available, here are a couple of ideas if you tire of eating it in pesto.

Garlic Mustard Oil with Red Pepper Flakes

We basted a leg of spring lamb with this garlic mustard oil as the lamb was roasting in the oven. After the roast was done, we used the mildly garlicky drippings as the base for a sauce for the meat. This perfumed olive oil can also be used to baste roast chicken, replacing butter. It gives a crackly, salty, mild garlicky tang to roasts and meats but is also nice in a salad, on poached fish, drizzled over pizza, or stirred into mashed potatoes. ❧ **Makes 2 cups**

1½ cups extra-virgin olive oil
2 tablespoons salt
1 tablespoon red pepper flakes
1 tablespoon sugar
1½ ounces (2 cups) garlic mustard leaves, finely chopped

In a small pot, heat the olive oil until a chopstick dipped in it sizzles but the oil is otherwise still (140°F). Remove from the heat. Add the salt, red pepper flakes, sugar, and garlic mustard. Let rest for a few hours at room temperature, then store in the refrigerator in an airtight container for up to a month.

Garlic Mustard Eggplant Dip

The garlic mustard leaves add a green and garlicky punch to a smooth eggplant spread. Slather it on crackers, pita bread, or crisp vegetables.

 Serves 4

> 2 medium or 1 large eggplant (18 ounces)
> ¼ cup sesame tahini
> ¼ cup fresh lemon juice
> ¼ cup extra-virgin olive oil
> Hot sauce
> Salt
> 1½ ounces (2 cups) garlic mustard leaves, thinly sliced

1. Preheat the oven to 370°F.

2. Bake the eggplants whole in the oven for about 20 minutes, or until they are soft to the touch and look collapsed and wrinkled. Cut the eggplants in half lengthwise and remove the pulp with a spoon, discarding the skin. (Eddy also removes any large clusters of seeds for a finer consistency.)

3. In a food processor or blender, puree the pulp with the tahini, lemon juice, and olive oil until a bit chunky or smooth, depending on your preference. Season with hot sauce and salt. Pour into a medium bowl and let cool. Stir in the garlic mustard leaves.

DANDELION *Taraxacum officinale* (SEE PHOTOGRAPH PAGE 18)

Foraging level: Green

Form: Herb (young leaves before flowering, flower)

Found in: Lawns and sunny open spaces throughout the United States and Canada. Originally from Europe and naturalized in Asia.

Growth habit: Grows singly from a large taproot, initially forming a basal rosette; the flower forms on an upright stem.

Key characteristics: Familiar to the French as *pissenlits* or *dents de lion,* dandelions have leaves with sharp triangular points that look like the teeth of a lion. If you tear the stem, you will see a milky sap.

Harvest tips: Pinch or cut off young green leaves before flowering. If using the flowers, it's best to pick them on a sunny day when they are open.

The dandelion's yellow face blooms for only a few short weeks in spring. Yet everyone seems to know the dandelion as the bane of the perfect lawn. Every weekend across urban parks and suburban backyards, countless hours, gallons of pesticides, and lawn care dollars are spent trying to eradicate this weed. Since I have been foraging I have completely changed my attitude about the dandelion—it is easy to find, identify, and pick with no fuss or care, and now I have learned delectable ways to cook and enjoy them.

Maybe our aversion to dandelions is due to their bitter reputation. I remember my mother serving us dandelion salad in the sixties out of a Euell Gibbons book (*Stalking the Wild Asparagus*)—and sure enough, the greens were tough and bitter. But just as good coffee is only slightly bitter with many more complex flavor notes, prepared properly, bitter greens are relished as a delicacy around the world, known as "wild mountain" greens for Koreans, Japanese, and Chinese; as wild greens for French, Italians, and Eastern Europeans; and as "bitters" to Swedes.

DANDELION FLOWERS

Surprisingly, unlike the bitter bite of the leaves, the flavor of the dandelion flower is mild, floral, and sweet. The flowers open with the sunshine and close when the sun goes down or it is rainy. So even though they will close up in the refrigerator, their goodness is still stored inside. If you want them fully open, try to pick them within a few hours of cooking.

Dandelion Leaves, Poached Eggs, and Bacon Bits

A classic French bistro-style dish, this salad combines the bite of the dandelion leaf with the creamy softness of poached egg. Eddy likes to cook half of the dandelions in the bacon drippings and leave the other half raw to bring out more flavor and texture. If you don't want to serve poached eggs for a leisurely brunch, feel free to soft-boil them all at once instead. ✒ **Serves 4**

> 1 pound small to medium Yukon gold potatoes
> Salt and freshly ground black pepper
> 2 tablespoons distilled white vinegar
> 8 slices bacon
> 2 tablespoons chopped shallots
> 1 tablespoon red wine or sherry vinegar
> 2 ounces (1½ cups) young dandelion leaves,
>   torn into bite-size pieces
> ¼ cup grapeseed or olive oil
> 4 large eggs

1. In a medium pot, cover the potatoes with cold salted water, bring to a boil, and cook for about 20 minutes, or until a fork will pass through a potato. Drain and let cool slightly. Peel the potatoes while still warm and then cut into chunks.

2. In a large skillet, cook the bacon until crisp. Remove the bacon, drain on paper towels, and tear or cut into smaller pieces. Reserve 1 to 2 tablespoons of the drippings in the skillet. Return the bacon to the pan, add the shallots, and cook for 1 minute over medium-high heat, or until the shallots are softened. Add the red wine vinegar and cook for 2 minutes, or until the liquid has reduced. Add half of the dandelion leaves and the potato and cook, stirring, for less than 1 minute, just until the leaves have wilted.

3. Meanwhile, fill a large saucepan with 4 cups water and add 1 tablespoon salt and the distilled vinegar. Bring to a boil over high heat, then reduce the heat so that the water simmers gently.

4. Remove from the heat and transfer to a large bowl. Add the remaining raw dandelion leaves, toss with the oil, and season with salt and pepper. Divide among individual bowls.

5. Crack one egg into a ramekin or teacup without breaking the yolk. Gently pour the egg into the simmering water and quickly repeat for the other eggs. Simmer the eggs for 4 to 5 minutes, or until the white of each egg is set but the yolk is still runny. With a large slotted spoon, remove each egg from the water and transfer to the top of a salad. Serve immediately.

OSTRICH FERN *Matteuccia struthiopteris*
Foraging level: Yellow

A native herbaceous plant that grows in moist open woods in the northeastern and central United States and Canada, ostrich fern fiddleheads are the young curled fronds that first peek out and eventually unfurl to become the toxic fern leaves. The fiddleheads are big, smooth, with no fuzz or hairs. Fiddleheads have become quite the rage now in farmer's markets and on restaurant menus, but we find that the flavor is not that unique compared with any other green cooked vegetable. Additionally, the plant is not all that easy for the novice to identify (particularly at the fiddlehead stage), and certain ferns are beginning to decline in the woodlands. To identify, it may be easier to plant the right species in a shady spot or observe them later in the year to see that they grow 2 to 5 feet high and the leaves look like a feather with one main stem (not branched). Its growth habit is to spread underground by rhizomes. That being said, ostrich fern is one of the more commonly found and abundant of ferns. If you would like to try some, Eddy recommends stir-frying or blanching them in salted water for 2 to 3 minutes.

Dandelion Flower Jelly

If you have a meadowful of dandelion flowers, bottle up their sunshine and make this sweet jelly that has the flavor of amber honey and notes of chamomile. You can put it in the refrigerator and serve it right away, but the flavor gets deeper if you wait a few weeks. This jelly will not become stiff; it is meant to remain runny so it can be drizzled. Jean-François Bruel, executive chef of Daniel, fondly remembers his *maman* making dandelion flower jelly when he was a kid in France. Since it is quite sweet, serve it drizzled over pear slices with shaved Parmesan cheese or Gruyère, or spread on toast or pancakes, or, as Ms. Amon's third graders loved it, on plain old saltines. ❧ **Makes 4 cups**

> 7 ounces (about 6 cups) dandelion flowers, plus 5 flowers
>   separated into petals
> 1 orange, peeled and cut into thick slices
> 1 cup sugar
> 1 teaspoon pure vanilla extract
> 1 tablespoon fresh lemon juice
> 1 (1¾-ounce) package powdered pectin

1. Set a small plate in the freezer for testing the jelly later. Using scissors, snip off the bottom green bump that holds each flower together (the peduncle) as well as much of the green leaf crown joined to the flower.

2. In a large pot, bring 3 cups water to a boil over high heat. Add the dandelion flowers (setting aside the ones separated into petals) and orange, reduce the heat to low, and simmer for 5 minutes. Turn off the heat and let infuse for at least 1 hour and up to 5 hours. Strain the liquid through two layers of cheesecloth or a jelly bag into a medium saucepan. Wring the cloth hard with two hands to squeeze all the liquid into the pan.

3. Bring the liquid to a boil over high heat. Add the sugar and return to a boil. Add the vanilla extract and lemon juice. In a heat-safe 1-cup measure, vigorously mix the pectin with ¼ cup of the hot liquid so that the pectin does not become lumpy. Add the pectin mixture to the pan and boil for 3 minutes. Check the consistency by dropping a teaspoon of the hot jelly onto the chilled plate and leaving it in the freezer for 10 seconds. When you run a finger through the gel on the plate it should form a trail or otherwise achieve the consistency you are looking for. If it does not, continue to boil for 2 more minutes. Remove from the heat and stir in the tiny petals. Pour into glass jars and refrigerate.

GOLDMOSS SEDUM *Sedum acre*

Foraging level: Green

A common North American ornamental groundcover or hanging basket plant that readily escapes and naturalizes, this particular sedum is an unexpected little treasure that grows low like a light green mossy carpet and blooms with little star-like yellow pixie flowers, each with 4 to 5 petals. On closer inspection, you'll notice the little crown shapes and the smooth, succulent texture—like cactus but without spines. Also like cactus, it retains and stores water in its leaves. Originally from Europe, the name *goldmoss* may be just an alias for its longer eighteenth-century name: welcome home husband though never so drunk. It is true that the smooth, fleshy, crown-shaped leaves have a nice mild taste, and when you eat a little cluster you get a tiny burst of juice (full of drink) in your mouth. The fresh green succulent taste of these miniature crowns is fantastic when used to balance rich, fatty meats or fish. Harvest by cutting off the top 1- to 2-inch crowns (either before or in flower) and not the bleached stems.

Braised Beef, Dandelion Leaves, and Clear Noodles

In cool weather, many Asian families enjoy rustic "hot pot"–style meals, where everyone gathers around a large pot set over a one-burner gas stove (like a camping stove). Everyone digs into dinner, which often includes a wild green or other dark leafy vegetable. Eddy was inspired by these traditions to meld the fatty and sweet qualities of beef and clear rice noodles with the sharper dandelion leaves. ❧ Serves 4

1 tablespoon salt
3 tablespoons toasted sesame oil
1 (3-ounce) package thin, clear rice noodles, such as vermicelli
12 ounces beef tenderloin, cut into $1/2$- to 1-inch cubes
4 small spring onions or scallions, white and light green parts, sliced
1 ounce (1 cup) snipped wild garlic greens (optional)
2 tablespoons light soy sauce or tamari
$1/4$ cup mirin
6 ounces ($4^1/2$ cups) young dandelion leaves
1 tablespoon sugar
8 ounces firm tofu, drained and cut into 1-inch cubes
Freshly ground black pepper

1. In a large pot, bring water, the salt, and 1 tablespoon of the sesame oil to a boil. Add the noodles and cook for about 2 minutes, or until soft. Drain and reserve.

2. Heat the remaining 2 tablespoons sesame oil in a large skillet over high heat. Add the beef and sear until browned on all sides, about 2 minutes. Add the spring onions and wild garlic greens, if using, turn down the heat, and cook for 1 minute. Add the soy sauce and mirin, followed by the dandelion leaves and sugar. Gently stir so that the large volume of dandelion leaves can cook evenly. Add the noodles and tofu and gently stir so that the noodles soak up the gravy and turn a light brown. Season with pepper and serve.

Dandelion Flower Tempura
with Savory Dipping Sauce

A change from the usual fried shrimp or vegetable tempura, the flowers, fried in a light batter (low gluten or gluten free), become pillowy light and sweet. We leave on the green parts at the bottom of the flowers for a tiny bit of bite; the savoriness goes well with the soy-dashi sauce. We can't get over how good these are—and how all too soon the dandelion flower season is over until next year. ❧ **Serves 4**

> 2 cups bonito flakes
> 3 tablespoons light soy sauce or tamari
> 3 tablespoons mirin
> ½ cup tempura flour (available at Asian and gourmet groceries), or more if needed
> Vegetable oil
> 25 dandelion flowers, stemmed

1. Put the bonito flakes in a bowl and pour in ⅔ cup warm water. Let steep for at least 5 minutes. Strain, discard the flakes, and reserve the dashi.

2. Pour the dashi into a small saucepan and add the soy sauce and mirin. Simmer over low heat for 5 minutes. Turn off the heat and let cool. Pour into 4 individual dipping sauce bowls.

3. Lightly stir about ¼ cup very cold water into the flour until just combined. Do not overmix. Adjust the proportions of water and flour, if needed, so that the mixture is still a little lumpy, with enough liquid so that it is not a solid mass but not watery.

4. In a large frying pan, pour enough oil to reach ½ inch up the side of the pan, and turn the heat to high. Test the temperature by dropping a drop of batter into the oil. It should sizzle. Dip batches of the dandelion flowers in the batter, up to 8 at a time. Lightly drop a batch of the coated flowers into the oil. Fry for 1 minute or less, or until light brown, turning the flowers so that they cook evenly. Transfer to a paper towel. Repeat, cooking the remaining flowers in batches. Serve immediately with the dipping sauce.

ORANGE DAYLILY *Hemerocallis fulva* (SEE PHOTOGRAPHS PAGES 19 AND 26)

Foraging level: Green

Form: Herb (shoots, buds, flowers)

Found in: Sunny and part-shade gardens, roadsides, moist streamsides, and old farmsteads throughout most of the United States (except California) and Canada.

Growth habit: Upright stem, spreads through rhizomes.

Key characteristics: The shoots look like little two-dimensional smooth lime green fans and have underground connected roots (rhizomes)—*not* bulbs, like the toxic daffodil, which looks somewhat similar. The poisonous but uncommon false hellebore *Veratrum viride* shoot looks similar but is more triangular in the cross-section and also has greenish nonlily-looking flowers. To be sure you are harvesting daylilies and not another plant, pick only in a spot where you have seen the distinctive flowers growing: Daylily shoots become long, basal, swordlike leaves and long leafless stems bearing oblong buds that open to unspotted orange-red flowers. When you cut off a shoot, it will have a mild leek aroma.

Harvest tips: Choose shoots that are 10 to 12 inches high with stems thick enough to have a structure that won't fall apart when cooked. Once they get tall and leggy, up to 2 feet or so, usually around the time the trees leaf out, they become too stiff for cooking. With scissors, cut off the shoots while young and still tender. Snip close to the bottom, where it is white and you can see rhizomes that join the shoots together, not bulbs. Cutting a number of shoots out of your garden bed does not harm the plant but instead helps them thrive and reduces crowding.

I can't help but notice the lime green shoots of the orange daylily as they stand out in the somewhat barren landscape of early spring. I bring some home and my Chinese father-in-law is excited to see them, as all his life he has eaten them dried but never seen them fresh, actually growing. After such a great reaction I decide I must bring some in to Eddy as well. He is immediately intrigued by their color and fan shape. Later that day he sends me an email: "Tama!!! It tastes like a cross between a mild leek and a French bean." He has already tried the shoots grilled, fried, boiled, and poached.

Grilled Daylily Shoots with Pine Nuts, Parmesan, and Balsamic Vinegar

You wouldn't guess it, but when cooked the shoots melt down like a scallion and turn a dark emerald green with a mild, clean taste. We were having some neighbors over for a casual dinner and, in the middle of the day when they were out, I snuck over and picked some daylily shoots from the hundreds in their beds. At dinner, they raved about the new ingredient and wanted to know at what farmer's market I had found them. ☙ **Serves 4**

8 ounces 12-inch daylily shoots (you will need about 25; use the entire fans and do not pull apart)
¼ cup plus 1 tablespoon extra-virgin olive oil
Salt and freshly ground black pepper
1 (3-ounce) block Parmesan cheese
⅓ cup toasted pine nuts
1 tablespoon balsamic vinegar

1. Toss the daylily shoots in 1 tablespoon of the olive oil. In a medium skillet (or grill pan) over medium heat, cook the shoots for about 5 minutes, or until wilted and tender. Season with salt and pepper. Transfer to plates.

2. Scatter large shavings of Parmesan (use a vegetable peeler) and the pine nuts over the top of the daylilies; drizzle with the vinegar and remaining ¼ cup olive oil.

Sautéed Daylily Shoots with Miso Dressing

This Asian-inspired recipe for these greens is a little sweet and a little salty, the perfect match for a simply cooked piece of fish. ❧ **Serves 4**

1 handful bonito flakes (½ ounce), optional
4 generous tablespoons (3 ounces) dark or regular miso paste
¼ cup plus 1 tablespoon extra-virgin olive oil
2½ tablespoons toasted sesame oil
2 tablespoons mirin
2 tablespoons rice vinegar
2½ tablespoons toasted sesame seeds
8 ounces 12-inch daylily shoots (you will need about 25; use the entire fans and do not pull apart)
4 ounces soft tofu, cut in about ½ inch cubes, optional
2 to 3 dashes of Tabasco or other hot sauce

1. Infuse the bonito flakes in 1 cup hot water for about 5 minutes. Drain off the bonito and reserve ⅓ cup of the liquid (also called dashi).

2. In a measuring cup, lightly whisk the dashi with the miso, ¼ cup of the olive oil, sesame oil, mirin, and rice vinegar. Stir in the sesame seeds.

3. Toss the daylily shoots with the remaining 1 tablespoon olive oil. In a medium skillet (or grill pan) over medium heat, cook the shoots for about 5 minutes, or until wilted and tender.

4. Toss the daylily and tofu with the miso dressing, add dashes of Tabasco, and serve.

THE MUSTARD FAMILY

The mustard family is entirely edible and includes familiar farm vegetables such as cabbage, broccoli, turnips, and kale, which originated in Europe and Asia. Asians eat a lot of mustards (such as bok choy and mizuna greens) stir-fried with ground meat and served with chili bean sauce and noodles or rice. Many of our favorite flavors of spring are wild members of the mustard family: the cardamines, dame's rocket, yellow rocket, brassicas, and shepherd's purse. There are many more species, and some will hybridize and cross with each other naturally. Just as whole-wheat bread or brown rice has a heartier, slightly bitter, saltier, and more complex flavor than white bread or rice, so, too, do wild mustard greens.

YELLOW ROCKET *Barbarea vulgaris* (SEE PHOTOGRAPH PAGE 22)

Foraging level: Green

Form: Herb (young leaves)

Found in: Moist fields and open disturbed lands throughout the United States and Canada (excluding Texas).

Growth habit: Starts as a basal rosette of leaves; eventually forms an upright stalk with leaves and buds.

Key characteristics: The basal rosette has dark green, smooth, curved lobed leaves; yellow flowers have four petals. The taste is cabbagey with an end bite. You can also substitute the early yellow rocket *Barbarea verna*, which looks very similar but has slightly narrower leaves that lack the three-lobed leaflet at the end; it tastes more like watercress, with less bite.

Harvest tips: Dig out young plants by the taproot before they flower or pull off the leaves.

The first year that I saw yellow rocket in bloom and brought Eddy some leaves, he grimaced at how tough and bitter it was. But my visiting Chinese mother-in-law cooked all of it and also preserved some of the leaves in salt—they were delicious, so I made a note next year to bring him the very young leaves before flowering, which would be more tender and less bitter, and more to his palate.

Early the next spring I spotted some shiny green yellow rocket leaves peeking out here and there from under the bleached winter grasses in the dry meadow. I dug out the rosettes with a small trowel and chopped off the muddy roots to leave behind in the field. Eddy stir-fried the leaves and I smiled at his reaction: "They taste good! Almost like popcorn kernels and then at the end a slightly—enticingly—bitter bite."

FIELD MUSTARD *Brassica rapa* (SEE PHOTOGRAPH PAGE 19)

Foraging level: Green

Form: Herb (leaves, flowers)

Found in: Sunny fields throughout the United States and Canada.

Growth habit: Tall, upright, invasive.

Key characteristics: Field mustard is commonly found standing several feet high with four-petaled yellow flowers; smooth waxy green pointy leaves clasp the stem. The leaves can have a whitish bloom like you would see and feel on a cabbage. It should taste cabbage-like.

Harvest tips: Pulls out easily or can be cut in half at the stem.

When I saw the yellow mustard flowers begin to bloom, I walked out into the field to see whether I had missed the season for yellow rocket, which is just plain bitter after flowering, or whether I was just in time for the field mustards, which taste great when in flower. I gave a whoop and in just fifteen minutes I had an armful of field mustard and carried it back like a large bushel of wheat.

Eddy was delighted with the taste of the leaves and he quickly stir-fried them with shrimp. The flowers are also delicious, with a mild flavor of cabbage and turnip with bitter notes and mustard at the end. Eddy took to scattering the golden flowers on dinner specials at the restaurant.

Wild Mustard Greens and Chorizo Wild Rice

This dish makes a one-pot meal, hearty and loaded with flavor. The taste of the mustard volleys back and forth between that of the chorizo and wild rice. My daughters liked this so much they made it several times during our recipe testing, substituting different mustards for variety. ⌣ **Serves 4**

> 1 cup wild rice
> 2 cups low-sodium chicken stock or broth
> 3 sprigs of thyme
> 2 garlic cloves, 1 whole and 1 chopped
> 1 tablespoon olive oil
> 2 ounces spicy cured chorizo (not raw sausage), cut into $1/2$-inch dice ($1/2$ cup)
> 2 small onions, diced
> 3 ounces (2 cups packed) wild mustard or yellow rocket leaves
> Pinch of salt
> 1 tablespoon sherry vinegar

1. In a medium pot, combine the rice, chicken stock, 2 cups water, the thyme, and the whole garlic clove. Cook over low heat, stirring occasionally, for 1 hour, or until the rice is tender.

2. In a medium skillet, heat the olive oil and chorizo over medium-high heat for 1 minute. Add the chopped garlic and the onions and cook for 2 minutes, or until softened. Stir in the mustard leaves, season with salt, and cook for 3 minutes. Add the sherry vinegar.

3. When the rice is done, stir the mustard and chorizo mixture into the wild rice and broth. Serve hot.

Wild Mustard Greens and Shrimp Wonton Soup

The soft chewiness of the soup dumplings and the sweet shrimp tango back and forth with the bite of the mustard. The quality of the shrimp matters here; Eddy chooses small, sweet Maine shrimp in season. My husband said the wild mustard makes these better than dumplings he eats in Hong Kong. Serve some rice vinegar on the side as a dipping sauce, which rounds out the flavors of the sweet shrimp and slightly bitter mustard. ∾ **Serves 4**

2 generous handfuls (1 ounce) of bonito flakes
2 tablespoons toasted sesame oil
1 small onion or spring onion, chopped
1 garlic clove, chopped
Pinch of red pepper flakes
3 ounces (2 cups) wild mustard leaves, plus more for the broth
2 tablespoons light soy sauce or tamari
1 pound fresh sweet shrimp, shelled, deveined, and coarsely chopped
16 square wonton wrappers
1 large egg white or water

1. In a medium saucepan, bring 3 cups water to a boil. Turn off the heat, add the bonito flakes, and let infuse in the hot water for 15 minutes. Strain, discard the flakes, and reserve the dashi broth.

2. In a medium skillet, heat the sesame oil and cook the onion, garlic, and red pepper flakes for 2 minutes, or until the onion softens. Add the mustard leaves and cook for a few minutes until softened, adding a spoonful of the dashi broth and the soy sauce to keep the mixture from getting too dry. Remove from the heat, roughly chop, and let cool.

3. Stir the shrimp into the mustard leaf mixture. Set out several wonton wrappers on a smooth surface (keep the rest covered with a slightly damp towel so they don't dry out). Brush the wrappers with the egg white on the edges to seal. In the center of each wrapper, drop a large teaspoonful of the shrimp mixture.

Fold the wonton wrapper over the filling to form a triangle, sealing the edges. Bring the two points of the triangle to meet each other and press together, sealing with a little egg white. Repeat with the remaining wrappers and filling.

4. Bring the dashi to a boil, adding a few mustard leaves. Add the dumplings and lightly boil for 2 to 5 minutes, or until the wrappers become translucent and you can see the pink from the shrimp through the wrappers. Serve the dumplings in a soup bowl with the dashi.

RAMPS *Allium tricoccum* (also *Allium ursinum* in Europe)
Foraging level: Yellow

Ramps are a specialist native plant that grows in moist, rich woodlands of the northeastern and central United States. Also known as wild leeks, they have become an expensive trendy "gourmet" food. I carefully clip off a leaf here and there until I have just enough for a meal. Digging out the bulbs, instead of clipping, disturbs the ground as well as removes their primary source of regeneration. Ramps have a thick, smooth leaf 2 to 3 inches across, 8 to 10 inches long, elliptical in shape with an oniony flavor. Eddy likes to spoon marinated raw ramps in their sauce over sliced and grilled sirloin steak. Marinate 16 wild ramp leaves for a few days in a mixture of 1/4 cup light soy sauce or tamari, 1/3 cup rice vinegar, and 1/3 cup sugar.

GARLIC PENNYCRESS *Thlaspi alliaceum* (SEE PHOTOGRAPH PAGE 20)

Foraging level: Green Form: Herb (young leaves, stems) Found in: Sunny open fields, roadsides, and disturbed ground from Pennsylvania to North Carolina and spreading westward in the United States.	Growth habit: Starts as a basal rosette and shoots up a tall, thin stalk. Key characteristics: Smooth leaf texture, leaf clasps stem, garlicky smell.	Harvest tips: Pennycress pulls out easily. Snip off the top 5 inches of tender tops or, if the plant is more mature and the stems are stiff, pull the leaves off the stems.

This might seem like a small moment in the scheme of things, but it just goes to show how every year there are new wild plants to find nearby. Last spring, I saw masses of brilliant light green lining the road, and although I couldn't find the plant in any of my books, I could place it in the brassica mustard family because of its smooth leaf texture, the way the leaf clasps the stem, and that mustard garlicky smell (that fills up the back of the car!). It looked a little like this species and a little like that species. So I asked an expert botanist, and he said it looked like *Thlaspi alliaceum,* or garlic pennycress, which has bits and pieces of two different mustards. He had seen it once on the edge of farm fields; it came over from Europe to North Carolina in 1960. So he drove around looking for it and sure enough, for some reason this year it was springing out all over on roadsides, in yet unplanted cornfields, in backyards, looking, as he describes, like "a tall skinny thing, white flowers, smooth stems, leaves clasping at the base, bottom or basal leaves are entire or slightly lobed." When he crushes the leaves they "smell vaguely garlicky," and taste "oniony-garlicky."

Eddy was soon hot on the taste trail. His report: not just edible—delicious. The taste starts off with a spring pea flavor, then changes to toasted garlic, and ends up with a peppery cress. After convincing Jean-François that we were fine and healthy after eating the plant, Jean-François served up a daily special pairing the kick of the tips of the garlic pennycress with a smooth spring cress velouté.

Pennycress, Asparagus, and Mango Vinaigrette

This recipe got a "whoa!" from an Audubon naturalist friend—who I hadn't been sure would like the unusual combination of flavors. He then proceeded to made it with his kids, who explained to me that "whoa" translates to "awesome" in their family. ⬥ **Serves 4**

4 white or green asparagus spears, outer layer peeled,
    woody bottoms trimmed
1 ripe mango, peeled and seeded, a few shavings reserved
    for serving
Juice of 1/2 lime
1 1/2 teaspoons rice vinegar
2 tablespoons grapeseed or canola oil
Salt and freshly ground black pepper
2 ounces (2 cups) young garlic pennycress or mild mustard soft tips
    and leaves

1. Bring a medium skillet of salted water to a boil and cook the asparagus for 5 minutes, or until just soft. Remove immediately, let cool, and cut into 1- to 2-inch pieces

2. Puree the mango in a blender with the lime juice, vinegar, and oil, and season with salt and pepper.

3. Arrange the asparagus and pennycress on plates, spoon the mango dressing on top, and garnish with the reserved mango shavings.

CREEPING JENNY *Lysimachia nummularia* (SEE PHOTOGRAPH PAGE 18)

Foraging level: Green

Form: Herb (leaves, flowers)

Found in: Sunny areas, open disturbed spaces, garden beds, field edges, and forest edges throughout the United States and Canada (except for the Great Plains and Southwest).

Growth habit: Low, sprawling, creeping, aggressive.

Key characteristics: Very round yellowish green leaves sitting opposite along the trailing stem; brilliant yellow flowers at the stem and leaf joints in early summer.

Harvest tips: Cut off the tender 2- to 3-inch rosebud tips at the end.

I didn't know that this plant, also known as moneywort, was edible until I traced the species back to its roots in Europe, where it is served as a garnish in certain high-end restaurants. So when Eddy asks me to bring in "what is out there," I bring in some trailing stems, just when the green unfurled rosebud tips are growing out at the ends of the brown worn trailers from last winter. He chews thoughtfully. The stems are too fibrous, he reports, but the leaves have a charming round shape and a mild mozzarella-like taste. Later that day I get an excited message from Eddy: "Same thing but a hundred times better flavor when cooked briefly with a tiny bit of butter and chicken stock. It reminds me of the texture of pea shoots with a light bite to it."

Creeping Jenny Tips Sautéed with Peas

The addition of spring garden peas fortifies the creeping jenny's pea shoot flavor. This is hearty spring fare with a little heat from the red pepper flakes. ❧ **Serves 4 as a side dish**

> 1 cup low-sodium chicken stock or broth
> 2 tablespoons unsalted butter
> 2 spring or small onions, chopped
> 2 cups fresh shelled peas or frozen green peas
> 1 teaspoon red pepper flakes
> 1 tablespoon sugar
> 2 ounces (2½ cups) creeping jenny tips and small leaves
> Salt

1. In a small saucepan, bring the chicken stock to a boil.

2. Meanwhile, in a large skillet, melt the butter over medium heat. Add the onions and stir for 1 minute, or until soft and aromatic. Add the peas, red pepper flakes, and sugar, pour in the hot chicken stock, and increase the heat to high. Cook for about 4 minutes, stirring continuously, or until the liquid reduces and the peas are shiny and glazed. Finally add the creeping jenny and salt and cook for about 2 minutes, or until soft.

Creeping Jenny with Tomatoes and Mozzarella

Jenny's young tender leaves make for a little twist on a classic combination. ❧ **Serves 4**

> **3 large tomatoes, cut into 1-inch chunks**
> **12 ounces fresh mozzarella cheese, cut into 1-inch chunks**
> **2 ounces (2½ cups) creeping jenny tips and small leaves**
> **1 teaspoon red pepper flakes**
> **2 tablespoons balsamic vinegar**
> **3 to 5 tablespoons extra-virgin olive oil, to taste**
> **Salt and freshly ground black pepper**

Toss together the tomatoes, mozzarella, creeping jenny, red pepper flakes, vinegar, and oil in a bowl and season with salt and pepper. Let marinate for 15 to 30 minutes before serving.

FORAGER'S JOURNAL

As the temperature rises in early summer, I can't help but notice dazzling pairs of yellow flowers along jenny's stems. They look nice so I try a nibble; there is something surprisingly complex about the flavor, but I can't put my finger on it. I bring in a sample to Eddy. It is early in the day and as the chefs arrive, each comes up to him to say "Good morning, Chef," shake his hand, and hover for a minute or two, sneaking nibbles out of the bags. All munch, nod, and agree: The flower is wonderful, tasting like coriander, with citrusy notes. Bring more in!

CURLY DOCK *Rumex crispus* and (SEE PHOTOGRAPH PAGE 18)
BROADLEAF DOCK *Rumex obtusifolius*
(SEE PHOTOGRAPH PAGE 17)

Foraging level: Green **Form:** Herb (young leaves) **Found in:** Sunny disturbed areas, fields, roadsides, streamsides, and vacant lots throughout the United States and Canada. **Growth habit:** Basal rosette; later grows a tall flower stalk up to 5 feet, with nondescript green flowers and rust brown seed clusters.	**Key characteristics:** Dock has a long taproot; leaves are long and thick, with rough edges and a central vein. Curly dock's leaves are narrower and three dimensionally wavy on the leaf edges, whereas broadleaf dock has broader leaves, and the center vein can be more distinct and redder.	**Harvest tips:** Choose young tender leaves, no longer than a foot, and cut them off at the base. It's almost impossible to pull out the stubborn taproot. Once the center stem has begun growing, the leaves become tough and bitter. Chop roughly into 2- to 3-inch pieces before cooking.

I read that young dock leaves were eaten during the Great Depression and although that sounded a little like not-so-good tasting survival food, I thought we needed to try it out. So I brought some in to Eddy. When the two of us held it up for inspection in the bright lights of the kitchen, we both made a face—because even when young, dock looks very tough, like a brute of a leaf with an uneven complexion and an ugly red vein running down the center. Good thing this is all about taste, where the docks excel. Eddy compares the flavor to that of kale with a tiny bit of sour at the end. When cooked, it gets tender fast. A touch of cream makes the green quite presentable to guests.

Spaghetti with Braised Dock and Bacon

The cream really transforms the dock in this dish, making it taste almost nutty and giving it much more of a juicy, meaty texture than spinach or collards. My hungry daughters cooked and devoured this dish in an hour. ❧ **Serves 4**

1 (12-ounce) box of spaghetti
6 slices bacon
1 tablespoon unsalted butter
3 small onions, chopped
1 garlic clove, minced
6 ounces (4 cups) young dock leaves, roughly chopped
1 teaspoon red pepper flakes
Salt and freshly ground black pepper
1½ cups heavy cream
¾ cup freshly grated Parmesan cheese

1. Bring a large pot of salted water to a boil. Add the spaghetti and boil until al dente, 10 to 12 minutes, or according to the directions on the box.

2. Meanwhile, in a large skillet, cook the bacon until crisp. Transfer to paper towels to drain; tear into pieces once cool.

3. Pour off most of the fat from the skillet, leaving a thin layer. Add the butter and let it melt. Add the onions and garlic and cook over low heat for 2 minutes. Add the dock and red pepper flakes, season with salt, and cook for 3 minutes, or until the dock reduces greatly in volume and turns darker green.

4. Pour in the cream. Cook for a few minutes, until the cream reduces slightly, and then stir in the bacon.

5. When the spaghetti is done, drain it well and transfer to a large serving bowl.

6. Add ½ cup of the Parmesan to the dock mixture in the skillet and turn the heat to low. In about 10 seconds the cheese will melt. Pour the mixture over the spaghetti. Grind pepper over the bowl. Serve immediately with the remaining ¼ cup Parmesan.

Dock and Corn

The intensely smoky flavors of the paprika are essential in this dish in order to bring out the juiciness of the dock and sweetness of the corn. Back at the restaurant, front-of-the-house veteran Ginette Vrod was especially excited to find that a plant she had been battling as a weed in her garden could taste so good. ❧ **Serves 4**

> 2 tablespoons unsalted butter
> 1 medium onion, chopped
> 2 garlic cloves, minced
> 3 cups fresh corn kernels (from about 4 large ears) or frozen corn
> 5 ounces (3½ cups) young dock leaves, roughly chopped
> 1 teaspoon smoked paprika
> 1 teaspoon salt
> ½ cup low-sodium chicken stock or broth, or vegetable stock
> ½ cup heavy cream

In a large saucepan, melt the butter over medium heat. Add the onion and garlic and cook for 1 to 2 minutes, or until softened. Add the corn and dock and cook for 1 minute, then season with the paprika and salt. Add the chicken stock and cream and simmer until the liquid just coats the corn and dock, 5 to 10 minutes.

FORAGER'S JOURNAL

The group of American wildflowers called spring ephemerals should not be lumped with the edible crowd in the spring. These "specialist" wildflowers, such as trout lily, spring beauty, toothwort, mayapple, trillium, wild ginger, and solomon's seal, used to carpet the floors of woodlands in the northeastern United States. They emerge in early spring in that brief window before you can see the leaves on the trees and take advantage of this fleeting period to pollinate, take nourishment from the sun, and then die back to roots, runner, and bulbs, where they store their sugars and nutrients for the next spring. Many of these plants are declining in the wild and will not grow back if the soil around their roots is plowed or disturbed. Many are also slow growers; trilliums can take two years to germinate and seven to ten years to flower. When there are so many other lovely edible plants available in the spring, these species are better left treasured where found and not dug up or harvested from the wild.

SHEEP SORREL *Rumex acetosella* (SEE PHOTOGRAPH PAGE 21)

Foraging level: Green

Form: Herb (*not* vine; leaves)

Found in: Sunny lawns, fields, roadsides, and disturbed areas throughout the United States and Canada.

Growth habit: Basal rosette with creeping rootstocks; later grows a reddish seed stalk 1 to 2 feet high.

Key characteristics: Small distinctive spear-shaped leaves, with one arrowlike lobe and two pointy outer lobes.

Harvest tips: Cut the leaves at the base when the plant is 12 inches or shorter, and before the reddish seed stalk forms.

Acetosella means "little sour one," and this diminutive sorrel has an exquisitely tart taste. My daughter's schoolmates loved the way the small leaves look like fairy spears and rated them their #1 favorite "wild taste" to add to salads. Eddy agrees they look even prettier than the usual garden sorrel. He appreciates the flavor's depth and staying power, even after cooking.

Sheep Sorrel Risotto

The sorrel taste sings with a full lemony flavor in this creamy risotto.

Serves 4

2 tablespoons olive oil
1 medium onion, finely chopped
2 cups Arborio rice
1 cup dry white wine or vermouth
4$\frac{1}{2}$ cups low-sodium chicken stock or broth, heated
3 tablespoons mascarpone cheese (or substitute $\frac{1}{4}$ cup heavy cream)
5 to 6 ounces (about 3 cups) sheep sorrel leaves, roughly chopped
    into 2- to 3-inch pieces
1$\frac{1}{4}$ cups freshly grated Parmesan cheese
Salt and freshly ground black pepper

1. In a medium pot, heat the olive oil. Add the onion and cook for 1 to 2 minutes, or until softened. Add the rice and stir for another minute. Add the white wine and let it bubble away until almost completely absorbed. Add the hot chicken stock $\frac{1}{2}$ cup at a time, letting the rice gradually absorb the liquid before adding more. Cook for 20 to 25 minutes total, or until the rice is completely soft.

2. Add the mascarpone and sheep sorrel and stir for a few minutes, until the sorrel wilts and the cheese absorbs slightly. Remove from the heat. Mix in 1 cup of the Parmesan. The cheese will melt in a few seconds with the warmth of the risotto. Season with salt and pepper. Serve immediately, garnishing each serving with some of the remaining $\frac{1}{4}$ cup Parmesan.

COMMON BLUE VIOLET *Viola sororia* (SEE PHOTOGRAPH PAGE 22)

Foraging level: Yellow

Form: Herb (flowers)

Found in: Lawns and open disturbed areas throughout the eastern and central United States and Canada.

Growth habit: Low growing, basal rosette.

Key characteristics: Five-petaled multicolored flowers nod above heart-shaped leaves. It is very difficult to identify violets to the species level, so choose violets from open disturbed areas and not wet areas or forests so as to avoid specialist [foraging level: Red] or more rare species. Don't worry about matching the color exactly; although it is called blue violet, it has a range of colors.

Harvest tips: Clip off the violet flowers and keep in a box in the refrigerator for only a few days.

Violets are one of Eddy's favorites as well as mine. When I first brought them in, still with spring dew on them, he was excited and exclaimed, "It looks like a pea flower" and marveled at the natural varieties of color: deep purple, lavender, gray and blue, freckled, cream and yellow—almost like the United Nations of violets! With tender heart-shaped leaves and a sweet and simple flavor, these are like a little valentine.

We haven't included a lot of complicated recipes for violets because they pretty much speak for themselves without cooking. Eddy likes to include them in spring salads, though candying them can help to preserve a pinch of their very brief season.

Candied Violet Flowers

Our home-candied flowers did not look as nice as Eddy's, of which every petal was perfect, but it took only about 30 minutes to make 50, and the taste was unexpectedly good. The initial sweetness of the outer sugar soon melts into the delicate, fresh center of the flower.

Add a pinch of salt to 1 large egg white in a bowl and beat very lightly with a fork. Dip a clean paintbrush in the egg white and coat each fresh violet flower, front and back. Making sure that the flower is open, dip the flower into sugar, tapping off the excess. Lay each sugar-coated flower to dry for 24 hours at room temperature on a baking sheet. Store in an airtight container in a cool dark pantry. Use for decorating cakes or desserts.

FORAGER'S JOURNAL

One day as I am delivering my finds to Eddy in the restaurant lounge, Daniel spies us.

"Hello!" He beams. "How is foraging?" He can't resist opening a bag to see what's inside. He pops a violet into his mouth and then another and another, greedily.

"Yum! How nice."

"The season is only a few weeks," Eddy whispers to him low, in French, almost conspiratorially.

"Nice, could be easy to propagate, no?" Daniel remarks, still munching.

"Well, yes—although it may be not so easy," I chime in. "In the wild, it is spread by ants."

Daniel stands stock-still staring at me. "Unbelievable!"

It is true. The elaiosome, a lipid-rich covering surrounding the violet seed, has a scent that attracts ants, which carry the seeds into their underground dens. They consume the coverings over the cold winter months. The remaining seeds are thus "planted" in the underground tunnel, waiting to germinate the next spring.

KNOTWEED *Polygonum cuspidatum* (SEE PHOTOGRAPH PAGE 21)

Foraging level: Green

Form: Herb (small leaves, young stalks)

Found in: Shady and partly shady moist woods, roadsides, and streambeds throughout the United States and Canada (except for the Southwest and Texas, as well as much of the temperate world).

Growth habit: Invasive; knotweed grows in large clonal stands with spreading rhizomes. Stalks stand tall or slightly lean over.

Key characteristics: Thick succulent round hollow stalks, reddish at the joints, look almost like bamboo, growing 3 to even 9 feet high. Leaves alternate on the stalk and are simple (not toothed or lobed), with a point at the end.

Harvest tips: The season can be as short as 2 weeks. Select bendable, not woody, stalks and pull out or cut in half. Small, tender leaves growing from the center are best.

Known in Japan as *itadori*, the tiger's walking stick, the stalks of this invasive appear to rise out of the ground like an army of soldiers, growing straight up and in thick colonies. Eddy found the first year's sample of skinny stalks too woody. Even though the plants were young, they were not fleshy enough and did not easily bend to the touch. But the next year, I found a big stand of supple-stemmed soldiers in a floodplain forest. Success! These have a tart taste similar to rhubarb but with more texture and sparkle.

EDIBLE INVASIVE PLANTS

Invasive plants come from other parts of the world and spread rampantly in the U.S., disrupting the biodiversity of our landscapes. But many of them have great culinary value.

Invasive plants in this book are:

Aralia (Japanese angelica tree) (page 105)
Asian honeysuckle (page 137)
Asiatic dayflower (page 116)
Dame's rocket (page 118)
Daylily (page 82)
Field mustard (page 86)
Galinsoga (page 167)
Garlic mustard (page 72)
Japanese barberry (page 204)
Knotweed (page 102)
Lesser celandine (page 54)
Mile-a-minute (page 161)
Mugwort (Artemisia) (page 112)
Multiflora rose (page 151)
Narrowleaf bittercress (page 67)
Purple loosestrife (page 127)
Shiso (page 170)
Wisteria (page 118)

Knotweed Strawberry Crumble

This dessert is short on cooking time but long on sweet-tart flavor. It goes well with vanilla ice cream. ✒ **Serves 6 to 8**

KNOTWEED AND STRAWBERRIES
1¼ cups granulated sugar
½-inch piece of fresh ginger, peeled and quartered
1 teaspoon pure vanilla extract
¼ cup grenadine (optional)
14 ounces (about 1 large grocery bagful) small, tender knotweed stalks, preferably about 1 foot high and ½ inch in diameter, cut into 1-inch pieces
8 ounces fresh strawberries, hulled and sliced

TOPPING
½ cup all-purpose flour
½ cup (packed) light brown sugar
¼ cup granulated sugar
¼ cup old-fashioned rolled oats
Pinch of salt
6 tablespoons (¾ stick) unsalted butter, at room temperature

1. Prepare the knotweed and strawberries: In a large pot, bring 6 cups water to a simmer over medium-low heat with the sugar, ginger, vanilla, and grenadine, if using; cook for 10 minutes. Add the knotweed and simmer for 5 minutes. Set aside to cool. Drain the knotweed, discarding the ginger, and transfer to an 8-inch round gratin dish. Add the strawberries and toss to combine.

2. Preheat the oven to 350°F.

3. Make the topping: In a medium bowl, combine the flour, light brown and granulated sugars, oats, and salt. Mix in the butter. The mixture will be fairly dry. Spoon on top of the knotweed mixture in the gratin dish. Bake for 20 to 25 minutes, or until the crumble turns light golden. Serve warm.

Knotweed, Ginger, and Lemon Jam

I tend to dislike overly sweet jams, and this recipe fits the bill: not too sweet, with the unique tart and spicy mix of the knotweed and ginger. This jam is perfect to make if you miss the window for the younger stalks but have taller large ones, as long as they still bend to the touch. Spread thickly on a warm scone or piece of toast on a spring morning.

Makes 2 cups

2 pounds (about 2 large grocery bagfuls) knotweed stalks,
   woody bottoms trimmed, peeled and cut into ½-inch pieces
2 strips lemon peel, removed with a vegetable peeler
2 slices fresh ginger
1 tablespoon fresh lemon juice
2 cups sugar
¼ cup chopped crystallized ginger

1. In a large pot, combine the knotweed, lemon peel, ginger, and ½ cup water. Bring to a boil, reduce the heat, and simmer for 10 minutes. Break up the knotweed slightly by pushing on it with the back of a spoon. The consistency will thicken but will still be lumpy.

2. Turn the heat back up to high, bring to a boil, and add the lemon juice. Add the sugar, ½ cup at a time, stirring and returning to a boil after each addition. Cook over high heat, stirring, for about 10 minutes and no more than 20, until the jam is thickened and bubbling. Turn off the heat, remove the ginger slices and lemon peel, and stir in the crystallized ginger pieces. Ladle into 2 half-pint jelly jars and refrigerate.

ARALIA (Japanese Angelica Tree) *Aralia elata* (SEE PHOTOGRAPH PAGE 17)

Foraging level: Green

Form: Tree (leaf buds)

Found in: Hedgerows, thickets, and open woods in the northeastern, central, and Pacific northwestern United States and spreading.

Growth habit: Invasive large clonal stands.

Key characteristics: The aralia tree looks almost prehistoric, growing 12 feet high and sporting thorns and several-feet-long leaves. In early spring it appears as a thick grove of tall, bare, thorny, vertical 2- to 3-inch-diameter trunks.

Harvest tips: Once you find a bare grove, picking the right time to harvest is key, usually when the buds are 4 to 10 inches long and the leaves are still furled like little mopheads, with no hardened inedible thorns. Buds at the top of taller trees are more tender and less quick to form thorns in contrast to growth on small saplings. On less established stands, long-handled loppers work well most of the time. Or if you have two people, try our technique: We were quite successful having one person (wearing heavy gloves!) lunge up and hold down one of the skinnier trunks, while the second person plucked off the succulent bud at the end. I also collaborated with staff at Audubon to cut down a grove of this invasive tree at the right time for harvest. Once picked, the buds will keep in the refrigerator for up to a week.

To prepare aralia buds for cooking, examine them closely: At the very bottom, where you plucked the bud from the tree, there is a stiff woody part. Peel this off. If your buds are big and have several leaves emerging from them, break them apart into separate leaves and stems. If you spot some tiny thorns but they are soft and bend to the touch, they are still fine to cook up.

My eyes search the bare treetops for the wild buds, which are a delicacy in Japan (*tara no me*) and Korea, the taste prized over cultivated strains. The buds already look heavy and almost ready to harvest. I send some photos from out in the field to Eddy and he emails that he can't wait to touch them, so the next day I bring a large amount into the kitchen and watch the chefs exclaim over the primordial-looking giant buds and the long thorny bare sticks. Later Eddy sends an ecstatic two-word email: "Love it." He lightly fried them up in a tempura batter, then dipped them in ponzu sauce. Tasted "fantastic with a light aftertaste of sap and aromatic pine." Yun Young Lee, chef de partie, told me it made her so happy to taste it because for Koreans, aralia (*dureup*) is the symbolic taste of spring, and she hadn't been able to eat it since arriving in the United States years ago.

Tempura Fried Aralia Buds

The aralia is mild and a little sweet, with a texture that is almost like a very young stir-fried asparagus—some crunch but also soft. Use the recipe for Dandelion Flower Tempura with Savory Dipping Sauce (page 81), substituting about 5 aralia buds for the dandelion flowers. Break the buds into 4- to 6-inch-long pieces, as described on page 105, before frying.

FORAGER'S JOURNAL

The North American tree *Aralia spinosa* [foraging level: Yellow] looks similar and is sometimes interchangeably called the devil's walking stick or Hercules' club, but you will not find it in invasive stands. Stick with harvest of the invasive type instead, as picking off the tender buds will hinder the growth and viability of the tree.

Just-Poached Aralia with Mustard Vinaigrette

The aralia is crunchy and fresh like young asparagus but without the fibrous texture. Dipping it in the mustard vinaigrette enhances its flavor and adds lemony notes. Or serve it as the Koreans do, alongside a chili dipping sauce. ❧ **Serves 4**

> **9 ounces medium (4- to 8-inch) aralia buds (about 12),**
>   **prepared as described on page 105**
> **3 large eggs**
> **½ cup grapeseed or canola oil**
> **¼ cup white wine vinegar**
> **¼ cup Dijon mustard**
> **Tabasco**
> **Salt**

1. Bring a medium pot of salted water to a boil. Add the aralia and boil for less than 1 minute, or until slightly tender but still crunchy. Scoop out the aralia with a slotted spoon and drain well.

2. Have ready a bowl of ice water. Cook the eggs (in the shell) in the boiling water for 5 minutes, drain, and transfer to the ice water to cool. Peel the soft-cooked eggs and transfer to a blender or food processor. Add the oil, vinegar, and mustard and season with Tabasco and salt. Blend for about 2 minutes, or until thick and smooth.

3. Serve the aralia topped with the mustard vinaigrette.

SPRING

When the trees leaf out and the apple and cherry trees blossom, many people traditionally think that spring has arrived, although foragers know that there has been plenty of green plant life in the preceding months. Now, however, I can see a clear break, a shift in the terrain, when the early spring plants are fading or sending up flowers and the next wave of plants is arriving.

Once a plant flowers, the sugars go to the flowers and the greens become tougher and more bitter. So we switch to different leaves, such as the heady herbal and tea tastes of nettle and artemisia, or to the same family but later-blooming cardamines and mustards. And of course, there are all those flowers for Eddy to experiment with.

FORAGER'S JOURNAL

CAUTION: Poison ivy (*Toxicodendron radicans*) is found throughout the eastern and central United States and Canada. In the spring, poison ivy's three-leaf formation is reddish and shiny. But individual poison ivy plants can be quite variable, creeping on the ground, climbing like a vine, or even forming woody trunks. The easiest way to distinguish (and thus avoid) poison ivy from other three-leaved plants is by the sides of the leaf, which are not symmetrical; there will be one or more jagged "teeth" on one side of the leaf and a different number or none on the other. Also avoid vines with long straggly hairs; poison ivy vine hairs can give you the itch, too.

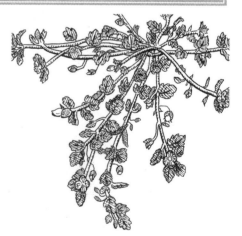

ARTEMISIA OR MUGWORT *Artemisia vulgaris*

(SEE PHOTOGRAPH PAGE 23)

Foraging level: Green

Form: Herb (young leaves before flowering)

Found in: Sunny disturbed ground, lawns, garden beds, roadsides, and fields throughout the United States and Canada (excluding Texas and the Southwest).

Growth habit: Invasive large stands; grows tall and straight, spreading through underground rhizomes.

Key characteristics: Soft, limp dissected leaves have many lobes (curved fingerlike projections) and, most important, the underside of the leaf is silvery white. Once picked, they have an herbal and chrysanthemum-like aroma.

Harvest tips: Cut the smaller, soft leaves and tops. To extend the season you can mow down mugwort and pick it when it grows back or pick small leaves that grow underneath the larger plants. Store in a plastic bag with a moist paper towel so that the leaves remain soft and do not shrivel or dry out. Mugwort does not keep for more than a few days in the refrigerator.

Despite the brusque name, mugwort is of an old and venerable family, from Eurasia, with well-known relations in the tarragon and daisy family. Since ancient times, mugwort has been used as a magical herb that wards off evil spirits and insects. There are several hundred different species of artemisia, some of which are edible and some more medicinal. The Japanese revere the beloved *yomogi,* eaten in sweet rice cakes filled with red beans and in tempura. Koreans use mugwort *sook* in rice cakes, soups, and pancakes. Make sure to get the right species as the common name *mugwort* is used interchangeably, and some species can be very bitter or inedible.

I bring bags of artemisia into the city and the fragrance trails after me on the pavement. Eddy likes the taste from beginning to end: a complex floral flavor, a bit of nettle, and a lingering hint of bittersweet at the end. When very young, it has a taste like white button mushrooms. As it matures but before flowering, it becomes more aromatic, taking on a smoky, wild taste. Eddy especially loves to use the leaves lightly fried as a tempura with Dover sole or monkfish.

Artemisia Soup

This easy soup shines the spotlight on the mildly herbal mushroomy taste of young artemisia. It is a lovely start to a meal. ⌒ **Serves 4**

> 1 medium onion or 3 small spring onions, sliced
> 3 tablespoons unsalted butter
> 2 garlic cloves, minced
> 10 medium white mushrooms (2½ ounces), sliced
> 1 large or 2 medium Yukon gold or russet potatoes (10 ounces),
>   peeled and cut into 2-inch chunks
> 6 cups low-sodium chicken stock or broth, or vegetable broth
> 4 ounces (8 cups) tender artemisia leaves
> 1 cup heavy cream
> Tabasco
> Salt and freshly ground black pepper

1. In a large pot, sauté the onion in the butter for 2 minutes, or until softened. Add the garlic and mushrooms and cook for 3 minutes, or until softened. Add the potatoes and chicken stock and bring to a boil. Add half of the artemisia leaves, turn the heat down to low, and cook until the potatoes are tender, about 20 minutes.

2. Add the cream and the rest of the artemisia to the pot and simmer for 10 minutes. Remove from the heat. In a food processor or blender, working in batches if necessary, puree until very smooth. Season with Tabasco, salt, and pepper.

GREENBRIER *Smilax rotundifolia*
Foraging level: Yellow

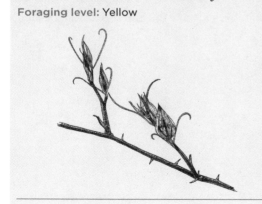

This vine with a woody base grows in openings in the woods, including forest trails in the eastern and central United States and Canada. The young roundish leaves and vines sprout out in the spring from the woodier and thorny base of the vine. The tendrils twine around and the delicate paper-thin, shiny, moss-green leaves, still-folded with a pointy top, melt in your mouth. Eddy thinks they make an interesting addition to a salad.

Artemisia Rice Crisps

Crispy rice is a familiar home-style Asian food. The Wongs say that it started as a way to use leftover rice that got stuck at the bottom of the rice cooker. But today chefs are making it from scratch and using it in stir-fries with hot sauce or pouring soup over just-fried crispy rice. The rice makes fun popping sounds as it cooks. 🐚 **Makes about 40 crisps**

> **1 cup short-grain or sushi rice**
> **2 ounces (4 cups) roughly chopped artemisia leaves**
> **½ teaspoon salt**
> **Grapeseed or canola oil for frying**

1. In a large pot, combine 1½ cups water, the rice, artemisia leaves, and salt. Simmer over low heat for 30 minutes, or until the water is gone and the rice is cooked through. Turn off the heat and let cool until slightly warm.

2. Line an 18 × 13-inch baking sheet with parchment paper. Spoon the warm rice onto the parchment paper. Place another sheet of parchment paper on top and press down to spread the rice to an even ¼-inch thickness. Remove the top sheet of parchment. The layer of rice should be thin but cover the bottom, about the thickness of rolled-out cookie dough. Dry thoroughly (in a warm spot, using a dehydrator, or in a 300°F oven for 50 minutes) until completely crispy. Break into 2- to 3-inch pieces. Store in an airtight container.

3. When ready to eat, pour grapeseed or canola oil into a small pot to a depth of ½ inch and heat over high heat. Test the temperature—a cracker should sizzle, but not burn, when dropped in the oil. Quickly fry the crackers in batches until golden and crisp, about 1 minute. Scoop out with a slotted spoon, drain on paper towels, sprinkle with salt, and serve.

STINGING NETTLE *Urtica dioica* (SEE PHOTOGRAPH PAGE 24)

Foraging level: Green

Form: Herb (leaves before flowering)

Found in: Fields, open woodlands, and path edges in rich soils throughout the United States and Canada.

Growth habit: Dense stands, tall and straight.

Key characteristics: Nettle is covered with tiny stinging hairs on its stems and leaves, which are opposite, rough, pointed, and toothed.

Harvest tips: Wear latex gloves and cut or pinch off the upper tips and leaves. Try to select plants that are 2 feet high or less, with leaves that look green and lush. Do not harvest once the nettle has begun flowering, when little green roundish "beads" on 3- to 4-inch strands will hang out of the joint of the stem and the leaf branches.

Eddy is intimately familiar with nettle as it has been used by Europeans for centuries as food, medicine, and tea, and in modern times is thought to help in controlling allergies and inflammation. The nettle has a deep but not sharp herbal flavor, with notes of celery and mint. It has great versatility in soups, sauces, pestos, and quiches. And we love it in Sheep Sorrel Risotto (page 99), substituting 6 cups (6 ounces) raw nettle leaves for the sorrel. In our house, my daughters know it is nettle season when they reach into the refrigerator without looking and get "stung" on the thumb. I now try to remember to keep the nettles out of the way in a thick garbage bag. Once the nettle is cooked or fully dried, the stinging magically and completely disappears.

WOOD NETTLE *Laportea canadensis*

Foraging level: Yellow

Stinging nettle has a cousin, the wood nettle *Laportea canadensis* (foraging level: Yellow), which has fewer stinging hairs and rounder and wider leaves, and is found in shady forests. Eddy found the taste interchangeable with stinging nettle, but we prefer to use the more abundant stinging nettle species.

Microwaved Nettles

Crispy nettle chips make a nice garnish to a salad or Chinese-style dinner, flash-fried and scattered around a plate of Szechuan chicken thighs or other stir-fried or braised meat.

Wearing gloves, pluck ½ ounce medium nettle leaves (about 40) and spread the leaves flat on lightly oiled parchment paper or plastic wrap. Grease the top side of each leaf lightly with a brush dipped in grapeseed oil. Cover a plate with microwave-safe plastic wrap, spread the nettle leaves in a single layer on the plate, and cover with another layer of plastic wrap. Microwave for about 2 minutes. Let rest for 1 to 2 minutes before removing the top layer of plastic. Season with salt and microwave again for about 1 minute, or until crisp. Lay the stiff leaves flat on a paper towel and pat dry to remove any excess oil.

ASIATIC DAYFLOWER *Commelina communis*

Foraging level: Green

SHOOT

Of Asian origin, this invasive herbaceous plant now grows in moist disturbed open areas throughout much of the United States and Canada (excluding California and Rocky Mountain states). The Japanese know it as *tsuyukusa,* or dewflower, since the flowers are open only in the early morning. The blue color of the flower evokes the sea and the sky. Eddy loves it both raw and cooked, for the soft crunchy texture and sweet mild taste. The young shoots grow low and have smooth leaves like little swords that wrap around the stem, which grows with little crooks in its joints. It needs to be carefully harvested from a nonpolluted site, but if you happen to have a colony of it growing in good conditions, pull out the shoots or clip off the tops down to the stems. Substitute in Chickweed with Sesame and Soy Sauce (page 65) or Grilled Daylily Shoots with Pine Nuts, Parmesan, and Balsamic Vinegar (page 83).

Nettle and Asparagus Pizza

The nettles cook down and become soft, similar to a deeply flavored spinach. They pair well with spring asparagus, making for a very flavorful vegetarian pizza. Try drizzling this with Garlic Mustard Oil (page 73). ❧ **Makes one 18 x 13-inch pizza**

> **4 quarts (about 1 kitchen garbage bagful) nettle leaves and tips**
> **Cornmeal**
> **2 tablespoons olive oil**
> **1 bunch (1 pound) medium asparagus, woody bottoms trimmed, cut into 2-inch pieces**
> **Salt and freshly ground black pepper**
> **½ pound store-bought refrigerated pizza dough**
> **8 ounces (1 cup) crème fraîche or sour cream**
> **4 ounces (1 cup) shredded cheeses, such as Parmesan, Swiss, mozzarella, and/or fontina**

1. Have ready a large bowl of ice water. Bring a large pot of salted water to a boil. Add the nettles and cook for about 3 minutes, or until wilted but still bright green. Drain the nettles and transfer to the ice water to cool. Drain well, squeezing the nettles with your hands to remove excess water, then roughly chop. You should have about 9 ounces.

2. Preheat the oven to 400°F. Dust an 18 × 13-inch baking sheet with cornmeal.

3. In a medium skillet, heat the olive oil over medium-high heat. Add the asparagus and cook for 2 minutes, or until bright green but still crunchy. Add the nettles, season with salt and pepper, and cook for 1 minute; remove from the heat.

4. Stretch the pizza dough to make a rectangle that fits onto the baking sheet. Spread the crème fraîche evenly over the dough, then distribute the nettle-asparagus mixture on top. Sprinkle with the cheeses and bake for 20 to 25 minutes, or until the crust is crispy and the cheese is melted and turning a bit brown in places.

WISTERIA *Wisteria floribunda* (SEE PHOTOGRAPH PAGE 24)

Foraging level: Green

Form: Vine, which may have a woody trunk if mature (flowers)

Found in: Sunny gardens and escaped to treetops in the eastern and central United States.

Growth habit: Invasive, twining over treetops, fences, and poles.

Key characteristics: Racemes of heavy, perfumed, pendulous bouquets of lavender, purple, pink, and white flowers can be 6 to 12 inches long or more. Alternate leaves have 7 to 13 leaflets; flowers open in sequence from top to bottom.

Harvest tips: Cut off a pendulous bouquet when the base of the bouquet is open but the younger flowers are still closed and look almost like pea flowers. Store for several days in a plastic bag in the refrigerator without water.

Eddy was attracted by the wisteria's color and discovered that the bottom closed (or half-closed) flowers are especially good and crunchy and hold up well without wilting in a vinaigrette. The open flowers have a heady fragrance and taste better raw than cooked.

DAME'S ROCKET *Hesperis matronalis*

Foraging level: Green

An invasive herbaceous plant that grows in dense stands on sunny forest and hedgerow edges throughout North America, the dame looks like a phlox, with showy purple, pink, or white flowers, but the dame blooms earlier and has four petals and not five, like the phlox. The leaves are alternately arranged and get smaller as you go higher on the stiff stem. They are narrow, toothed, hairy, and tougher in texture than many mustard leaves. But when cooked, the leaves no longer feel hairy and the taste is nice, with a bite but no hint of bitterness. The leaves and flowers make an excellent substitute for the greens in Wild Mustard Greens and Chorizo Wild Rice (page 87). My daughter Georgia cooked the purple flowers and leaves in fried rice with chopped ginger, chicken, and bacon bits.

Wisteria Flowers with Asparagus and Parma Ham

We passed by wisteria flowers every morning on the way to school and never would have expected their light and crunchy texture. This simple yet colorful dish of purple, pink, and green is a perfect blend of sweet, salty, and tangy. ❧ **Serves 4**

1 bunch (1 pound) thin asparagus spears, bottom 3 inches cut off
4 thin slices Parma ham, prosciutto or Serrano ham, torn into
    small pieces
5 tablespoons extra-virgin olive oil
3 tablespoons balsamic vinegar
Salt and freshly ground black pepper
1 ounce (1½ cups) wisteria flowers (from 2 to 3 bunches)

1. Have ready a large bowl of ice water. Bring salted water to a boil in a large deep skillet. Add the asparagus and cook for 1½ to 2 minutes, until bright green and crisp-tender. Drain the asparagus and transfer to the ice water to cool. Drain well and cut into 3-inch pieces.

2. In a large salad bowl, combine the asparagus and ham, pour in the olive oil and vinegar, and season with salt and pepper. Toss to coat. Add the wisteria flowers and serve.

Wisteria Flowers and French Beans

This simple lavender and green combination is crunchy and fresh, a perfect dish for spring. ❧ **Serves 4**

> 8 ounces green beans, ends trimmed and cut into 2- to 3-inch lengths
> 1 small shallot, finely chopped
> 3 tablespoons extra-virgin olive oil
> 2½ tablespoons sherry vinegar
> Salt and freshly ground black pepper
> 1 ounce (1½ cups) wisteria flowers (from 2 to 3 bunches)
> 8 ounces (1 cup) ricotta cheese (optional)

1. Have ready a bowl of ice water. In a medium saucepan, bring salted water to a boil. Add the beans and cook for about 4 minutes, or until bright green and still crunchy. Drain the beans and transfer to the ice water to cool. Drain well.

2. In a medium salad bowl, combine the beans, shallot, olive oil, and vinegar. Season with salt and pepper and toss to coat. Mix in the wisteria flowers and serve, topping each serving with a dollop of ricotta cheese, if desired.

SHEPHERD'S PURSE *Capsella bursa-pastoris*
Foraging level: Green

Found in sunny, poor, disturbed soils in roadsides and farm fields throughout the United States, these plants start as basal rosettes with dandelion-like leaves but no milky sap, and stretch up to bear seeds shaped like little triangles, or like the purse of a shepherd. The taste of the raw leaves is a bit peppery and nice for a salad. The alternately arranged leaves that clasp the stem are narrow and often quite small, so we generally prefer to use other plants instead, such as the cardamines. The shepherd's purse (*ji cai*) is sautéed with minced meat and tofu in Shanghai and is popular there in the spring when there is a custom of families going out together and picking wild herbs.

MORELS *Morchella* spp.

Foraging level: Yellow

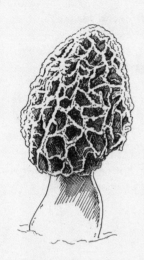

These delectable mushrooms grow in alkaline soils preferring ash, sycamore, and recently burned areas. They are found in various parts of the United States, but mostly in the Midwest and parts of the Northwest. Morels usually appear in early spring before the tree leaves emerge, but they can be finicky about where and when they choose to grow; some years can be abundant and others virtually barren. Morels grow to 3 to 6 inches and can be yellowish, brown, or black with a honeycomb top with ridges and pits. Some morels can accumulate a lot of sand in the ridges and for these you may need to wash and spin them more than five times to remove the sand. Eddy prepares morels in a gratin with parsley and also chops and mixes them into mashed potatoes.

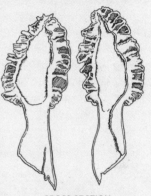

CROSS SECTION

Important ID note: Cut one in half lengthwise. It must be completely hollow and attached to a stalk. False morels are poisonous lookalikes that, when cut lengthwise, have chambers inside or are partly filled or stuffed.

SPRUCE *Picea* spp. (SEE PHOTOGRAPH PAGE 24)

Foraging level: Green

Form: Tree (young needles)

Found in: Forests in the northern United States and Canada but also widely planted in landscaping and Christmas tree farms.

Growth habit: Tall, upright, evergreen. The commonly planted Norway spruce stands 50 to 80 feet tall, with drooping branches; other spruces have more horizontal branches and largely conical forms.

Key characteristics: The needles are pointed, usually prickly (unlike balsam, hemlock, and the poisonous foliage of the yew, all of which have soft and blunt-tipped mature needles), and not joined together like pine tree needles. The needles are attached to little woody pegs that project out of the twig. It is the fragrant, sweet, and soft young tips that are fine in cooking (no tree chopping required). In midspring as the tree leaves are coming in, brown papery fingers start growing at the ends of the spruce needles. These scale off to reveal lime-green tips that look like small paintbrushes. The needles are not yet stiff and if you smell inside a tip, you'll get the sugary evergreen aroma.

Harvest tips: Clip off the soft, light green tips with a pair of scissors.

Eddy is fascinated by the way the tips are so soft and tender. He excitedly sends me iPhone photos of spruce trees as he walks to work through Central Park and is amazed that he never noticed them before. The taste is lemony, going to ginger and then ending with some pine notes. When cooked with a bit of sugar and infused, spruce can even begin to taste appley.

BLACK MEDICK *Medicago lupulina*

Foraging level: Green

You may have stepped on this low-growing common herbaceous plant, which spreads weedlike on the edges of lawns and roadsides throughout the United States and Canada, and thought it was clover. Though it has three small egg-shaped leaflets, the very tips of the leaf edges are a little bit toothed and uneven, and the plant has a longer hairy stalk. It also has a small yellow squat flower on a stem, smaller than that of a clover. The taste is satisfactory but not that interesting. It is best used as a small garnish or added to salads for its shape and texture.

Chilled Mango Soup
with Sweet Spruce Tips

We had never tried a dessert soup before but were pleasantly rewarded with this light, refreshing, and sophisticated version. The piney flavor and texture of the spruce tips balances the softness of the mango and the tapioca pearls. Add a scoop of mango sorbet to the center of the serving dish for extra flourish. ✲ **Serves 4**

¼ **cup large tapioca pearls**
¼ **cup sugar**
¼ **cup (about 40) soft spruce tips**
2 ripe mangos, peeled and diced

1. In a medium saucepan, bring 3 cups water to a boil. Add the tapioca, reduce the heat to low, and simmer for 25 to 30 minutes, or until the pearls are translucent and slightly gummy. Drain, then rinse to cool and prevent the pearls from clumping together. Refrigerate until needed.

2. In a small saucepan, bring 1¾ cups water and the sugar to a boil. Add the spruce tips and cook for 1 minute. Turn off the heat, pour the syrup and tips into a medium bowl, and refrigerate until cold.

3. Add the cooked tapioca pearls and diced mango to the spruce tips and syrup. Serve cold in dessert bowls.

CATTAIL *Typha latifolia* (SEE PHOTOGRAPH PAGE 23)

Foraging level: Yellow

Form: Herb (shoots, pollen)

Found in: Sunny wet open areas, swamps, pond edges, and ditches throughout the United States.

Growth habit: Large, upright, tall stands spread through rhizomes.

Key characteristics: Cattails are distinctive for their giant grasslike leaves and brown corn-on-the-cob-looking fruit. Since they can be confused with other shoots, look for the mottled ivory and brown stalks topped with white fuzzy seed heads left over from the year before to be sure you are getting cattails.

Harvest tips: Any plant growing in water should be carefully scrutinized to make sure that it is not in the line of runoff from any farm animals, spraying, fertilizer, pavement oil, or other pollutants. (I forage on a preserved swamp, with no building or person within sight.) Select a nice size cattail, at least the size of a broomstick handle at the bottom. Put both hands around the plant right above the water or mud. Jiggle it a bit and then firmly but gently tug it out. It will make the distinctive sound of a boot coming out of mud but pop off quite cleanly. The shoots are white and large.

It's a good thing I have on high waterproof boots, because I am soon almost up to my knees in soft mud. Red-winged blackbirds fly overhead but all else is quiet except for the suctionlike sound and pop as I pull out a shoot. I drop it into a large black garbage bag. The shoots with the leaves on them are the size of large golf clubs and do not fit in the refrigerator. If you are not going to cook the cattails right away, wrap paper towels around the bunch and secure with twine or plastic wrap. Place the bottoms in a jug of water and keep in a cool, dark location.

Eddy is very fascinated with the sculptural giant plant I carry in. I tell him that I heard the cattail is sometimes called the "Cossacks" asparagus and tastes like a heart of palm; he shakes his head at the notion of any comparison to asparagus. He continues to inspect the cattails closely, cutting off the tops and keeping the white 5 inches of tender bottom, peeling off the outer layers to get at the inner core. He holds one up to me and we each sniff in turn; the scent is sweet but familiar, like watery cucumber. He cuts off a few thin slices for us to taste, and indeed, it is like cucumber but with a different texture.

Pickled Cattail Shoots

This more tender variation on pickled cucumbers would match well as a side to potato salad, or in sandwiches. ∿ **Makes 1 pint**

> **5 cattail shoots**
> **1 cup distilled white vinegar**
> **¼ cup sugar**
> **1 teaspoon red pepper flakes**
> **1 teaspoon salt**

1. Trim the cattail shoots, keeping only the bottom 5 to 6 inches. Remove the outer layers until you get down to the smooth scallion-like heart.

2. In a medium saucepan, heat the vinegar, sugar, red pepper flakes, and salt. Add the cattail shoots and simmer over low heat for 1 minute. Remove from the heat and set aside to cool at room temperature before refrigerating for up to 1 month.

BLACK LOCUST *Robinia pseudoacacia*
Foraging level: Green

This tree, widely planted ornamentally, is native to the Southeast and has now escaped into the wild throughout the United States and parts of Canada. In midspring, the racemes bear cream white pendulous bouquets of flowers (looking much like wisteria) that bloom for a week or two with a heady but not overpowering fragrance. The tree has oval 1- to 2-inch leaflets and thorns on the trunks. The flowers taste slightly sweet but do not have as much flavor as wisteria; they have an interesting shape and a slightly crunchy texture, and are nice tossed on top of a fruit or light salad or scattered as a garnish for a dessert cake.

Summer Rolls with Cattail and Trout

The soft texture of the summer roll skin and trout is complemented by the smooth crunch of the cattail, creating a cool, tender dish.

❧ **Serves 4**

10 cattail shoots
1 smoked trout fillet (4 ounces), bones and skin removed, flesh
  shredded
¼ to ¾ cup mayonnaise, to taste
1½ teaspoons fresh lemon juice
Salt and freshly ground black pepper
4 spring roll (rice paper) skins
1 head soft lettuce, such as Boston, torn into 2- to 3-inch pieces
Fresh mint leaves, for serving

1. Trim the cattail shoots, keeping only the bottom 5 to 6 inches. Remove the outer layers until you get down to the smooth scallion-like heart. Have ready a bowl of ice water.

2. In a medium saucepan, bring salted water to a boil. Add the cattail shoots and cook for about 1 minute, or until just cooked. Drain and transfer to the ice water to cool. Drain well, pat dry on paper towels, and cut into small cubes.

3. Mix the cattail with the trout, mayonnaise, and lemon juice and season with salt and pepper. Lay the rice paper skins flat on a wet paper towel and wait for a few minutes until they soften. Arrange the lettuce pieces at the bottom of the rice papers and top with the trout mixture. Tuck in the ends of each rice paper and roll it up. Cut the rolls into 2-inch pieces and serve with mint leaves.

PURPLE LOOSESTRIFE *Lythrum salicaria*

Foraging level: Green

Purple loosestrife is an invasive herbaceous plant that grows in sunny moist areas and wetlands throughout the United States and Canada (excluding Florida and New Mexico). It forms dense stands, reducing the biodiversity and replacing other plants in ditches, pond edges, stream banks, and wet meadows. In late summer its beautiful magenta spikes of flowers are striking. But one plant may produce a million seeds a year, and the clumps also spread quickly through underground rhizomes. The plant looks like a mint with a square stem and opposite leaves, but tellingly lacks the distinctive minty smell. The young lance-shaped leaves of purple loosestrife taste like dock when sautéed and can be substituted for it (particularly as the season for loosestrife begins, when dock begins to toughen) in the recipes on pages 96–97. Since it may be difficult to spot before flowering, take note where you see large stands and then collect in late spring or early summer before it flowers.

SUMMER

Summer means long and golden unstructured days outside, close to the warm soil, watching an ant or two, meandering around in the garden, picking things and eating some, spitting out others. The wildflowers attract scores of foraging admirers by day—honeybees, bumblebees, wasps, butterflies, and hummingbirds—and in the evening a glimmering curtain of fireflies lights up the sky above the meadow. I avoid the midday heat and forage early in the dim light of the morning, often rousing some sleepyheaded bumblebee to tumble out of its bed as I pluck a flower or leaf still moist with dew. Sometimes the bees stow away to the city with me and later creep out to look around at the strange landscape.

For Eddy, one of the unique delights of summer foraging is the wild fruit. Instead of being large and fleshy and watery, wild berries are smaller than cultivated varieties but packed with intense flavor. The season starts with the mulberry, hanging cylindrically and curved like a beckoning finger, then turns to the dark, almost smoky wild huckleberries and blueberries, tart and nutty blackberries, sweet indigo juneberries, and shocking carmine red wineberries.

ELDERFLOWER *Sambucus canadensis* (see photograph page 27)

Foraging level: Yellow

Form: Shrub (flowers, blackish berries)

Found in: Sunny moist marshes, ditches, hedgerows, and stream and pond edges throughout the United States and Canada (excluding the Pacific Northwest); in the western United States, substitute blue elder *Sambucus cerulea.*

Growth habit: Straight, 5 to 13 feet tall; grows in clonal stands.

Key characteristics: Branches are arranged opposite each other; leaves are compound. The flat-topped cream-colored umbels of flower clusters usually bloom on the cusp of spring and summer.

Harvest tips: Cut clusters selectively, choosing ones in which the small flowers making up the clusters are fully opened but not browning on the edges.

My British friends love the European elderflower species, *Sambucus nigra.* On any late spring afternoon in London you can pop into a pub or fine dining establishment and find something elderflower on the menu, and in most grocery stores you can purchase bottled sparkling water flavored with the flower. Eddy likes the creamy, lacy flower clusters and thinks they smell like butter; the aroma and taste of *Sambucus canadensis* is very delicate compared with the stronger-flavored European elderflower.

White Chocolate Elderflower Lace

Normally I don't tend to like white chocolate. It tastes too sweet and bland, lacking that rich, well, chocolatiness that I expect in chocolate. But many times when I try Eddy's cooking, I change my mind about foods I don't usually like. So I didn't say anything when he told me he was excited to try elderflower with white chocolate. The results were amazing; the white chocolate is mild enough to let the subtle texture and floral tones of the elderflower shine through. But it is most important to use a high-quality white chocolate that will not overpower the delicate flavor of the elderflower.

This recipe is dedicated to our literary agent, Sharon Bowers, who, upon tasting a sample, tactfully and at the same time poetically suggested the name "lace," thereby ending our debate as to "tablet" (like a pad of paper or pill?) or "bark" ("sounds like an animal noise").

1. Cover an 18 × 13-inch baking sheet with parchment paper. Break 8 ounces good-quality white chocolate (such as Green & Black or Lindt; do not use chips) into pieces and melt in a microwave oven or double boiler. With a basting brush, brush the warm chocolate onto the parchment paper, brushing once horizontally, then vertically, then diagonally to coat the entire sheet of paper. Continue these thin layers until the chocolate is about 1 millimeter thick and you can no longer see through to the parchment. You will not use all of the chocolate at this point.

2. Spread 3 ounces (about 20 large clusters, or 4 cups) elderflower blossoms (washed very lightly and pulled off of the cluster stems) so they cover the top of the chocolate, pressing down with your hand so they lie flat.

3. Fill a pastry bag fitted with a very narrow tip with the remaining melted chocolate (you may have to lightly reheat it to maintain a liquid consistency) and quickly but steadily drizzle the chocolate over the top of the flowers, in different directions, like a spiderweb. The flowers should not be completely covered; you should still be able to see them peeping through the chocolate lace.

4. Put the baking sheet in the refrigerator for 1 to 2 hours, or until the chocolate has set. Flip the baking sheet over a cool work surface. Peel away the parchment paper and break or cut the flowers and chocolate into smaller pieces. Keep chilled until serving.

COMMON MILKWEED *Asclepias syriaca*
Foraging level: Yellow

This rough-looking, 2- to 3-foot herbaceous native plant grows in sunny fields and open disturbed areas throughout most of the United States and Canada (excluding California and the Southwest). It has big oblong rounded opposite leaves with a red vein down the center with very light salmon-pink drooping balls of flower clusters. The seedpods are edible, as are the boiled milkweed shoots (not to be confused with poisonous dogbane or butterfly weed, which also has seedpods although skinnier), even though the latex white sap is mildly toxic. Eddy finds it better to remove the pod and quickly blanch the tender seed bunches nestled inside in salty water. The shape of the young white seeds attached to each other looks a bit like a baby corn on the cob, with a taste similar to asparagus and ending with some ginseng notes. Milkweed leaves are a key survival link for the striped caterpillar of the monarch butterfly, which feeds only on milkweed. The flowers also provide important nectar for butterflies and bees. Given the importance of the milkweed in the ecology of our native landscapes, we prefer to forage other readily available plants.

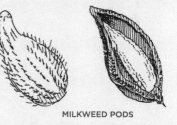

MILKWEED PODS

Elderflower Syrup

This cordial recipe intensifies much of the elderflower's floral perfume. It is adapted from our English–Northern Irish–Scottish family friends the Agnews, who continue their long-standing tradition of foraging for elderflower even though their glamorous sister broke her leg climbing over a neighbor's fence, caught in the act. When the flowers are at their peak, we make a batch and freeze it to use through the rest of the summer as the base for lemonade-like drinks or cool berry gelatins. ❧ **Makes 5 cups**

> **30 large elderflower clusters**
> **2 pounds sugar**
> **1 lemon, sliced**
> **2 generous tablespoons citric acid**

1. In a very large pot, combine the whole elderflower clusters, sugar, lemon, and citric acid.

2. In a separate pot, bring 5 cups water to a boil and pour it over the elderflower mixture, stirring well. Cover and set aside for 3 days, stirring once a day. Strain the liquid through cheesecloth or a fine strainer and reserve, discarding the solids. Pour into cup- or pint-size containers and freeze until ready to use.

ASIAN HONEYSUCKLE *Lonicera japonica*

(SEE PHOTOGRAPH PAGE 27)

Foraging level: Green **Form:** Vine (young leaves, flowers) **Found in:** Fields, roadsides, open forests, gardens, and disturbed areas throughout the United States (excluding the Pacific Northwest and the northern Great Plains).	**Growth habit:** Invasive, twining in masses over trees, fences, and hedgerows. **Key characteristics:** Leaves are opposite, egg-shaped, edges are straight but some younger leaves can be lobed; yellow and white flowers run in pairs along the stem, and are extremely fragrant.	**Harvest tips:** Pick the young leaves, cut or pull out the vines, and pluck the open flowers.

The flowers and buds of this Asian vine are a delicacy and considered an immune system boost in China, where they have been dried into tea since the ancient days of the Dowager Empress herself. There it is known as the mandarin duck honeysuckle, because the flowers skip along the stem in white or yellow pairs, like mandarin duck pairs that mate for life. The perfume of the honeysuckle is very powerful; the equally strong vine can overpower shrubs and small trees.

When Eddy sautéed the young leaves, they had a mild flavor with some slight bitter notes. They can be substituted for dandelion leaves in the beef recipe on page 80 or for mustard greens in the shrimp dumplings on page 88. As for the flowers, the best way to experience them is the simplest: Hold one over your open mouth, bite the end and suck out the drop of nectar; it is sweet and honeylike, the essence of summer.

Honeysuckle Granita

In the middle of an early summer heat wave, this refreshing granita, with subtle notes of honeysuckle, hits the spot. It is very nice with a tablespoon of chilled vodka or sake drizzled over the top of each serving. ◔ **Serves 8 or more**

> **1 cup honey**
> **2 ounces (4 cups) honeysuckle flowers, plus more for garnish**

In a large saucepan, bring 6 cups water to a boil. Turn off the heat and stir in the honey. Toss the honeysuckle flowers into the pot and let them infuse for about 30 minutes. Strain the liquid through cheesecloth or a jelly strainer, squeezing to extract as much of the liquid as you can (discard the solids), then pour into small flat trays (ice cube trays will do). Freeze for a few hours, until frozen solid. Remove and process coarsely in a food processor or blender for 1 to 2 minutes. Garnish with fresh honeysuckle flowers.

SERVICEBERRY OR JUNEBERRY *Amelanchier* spp.

Foraging level: Yellow

This small tree or shrub can be found blooming on wooded edges and hedgerows and in gardens in early spring throughout the United States but most prolifically in the Northeast and Canada. The poetic white-streaked pink flowers form 1/3- to 1/2-inch fruits that hang down later in the summer. Like blueberries, the fruits can be distinguished by the five-pointed crowns at the tips, and turn from red to purplish to blue-black. We like to harvest them when they are purplish and the size of a cultivated blueberry, with more sweet-tart complexity and not "just plain sweet." When cooked, the berries reveal their place in the rose family but also have incredible almond notes; the berries pair well with wild rose petals in a jam or coulis.

WILD MINT FAMILY WITHOUT THE MINTY TASTE: LAMIACEAE FAMILY

Walking through a lavender bergamot meadow or a stand of bee balm in bloom in midsummer, I can smell the heady herbal aroma, so I am surprised to find they are part of the large and prosperous mint family, but with no minty taste. Part of the American wild heritage, these plants are found less frequently now. They're easy to plant in your herb garden and need little care. Once they flower, the leaves are not as tender, but you can enjoy and sample their showy flowers.

BEE BALM *Monarda didyma* (SEE PHOTOGRAPH PAGE 25)

Foraging level: Red

Form: Herb (young leaves, flower petals)

Found in: Sunny gardens, moist woods, thickets, and fields in the eastern, central, and midwestern United States and south to Georgia.

Growth habit: Spreads slowly through rhizomes; tall, upright.

Key characteristics: Leaves grow opposite along a square stem; crushed leaves have a lemony herbal aroma; flowers are distinctively shaped and red. Eddy thinks the petals look like miniature lobster claws.

Harvest tips: Grow and harvest from your garden only; pick young leaves in spring and cut flowers in summer.

I handed over a small bag of bee balm leaves to Eddy and tried to spark his interest by telling him a story about the Boston Tea Party. "When the Americans threw the British tea overboard, they used the leaves of the bee balm, Oswego tea, as a substitute for the foreign British imported tea." My story went over like a lead balloon, but the taste went over like sun from behind a cloud; Eddy found it fresh and lemony. Daniel passed by and couldn't resist sneaking some out of the bag for a taste. "Mmm. Nice. Let's play with it."

Later in the summer the bee balm bears brilliant scarlet flowers with tubular petals that are ambrosia for the hummingbirds. I can hear the buzzing of their wings as they zoom in and around the garden. Plant a couple in a sunny spot and keep them well trimmed by using the leaves in a salad or on top of cooked shrimp with cocktail sauce as a finger food.

Bee Balm Spring Rolls with Lettuce and Dipping Sauce

Crunchy, lemony, minty . . . Chef Eddy's staff gave it a "three thumbs up" (don't ask me who has the extra thumb), and so did we. It's hard to believe that there is no lemon in the dish, but the lemony taste lingers around your mouth longer than a lemon, maybe because it is herbal rather than citrus. ☙ **Serves 6**

8 ounces lump crabmeat
¼ to ⅓ cup mayonnaise, to taste
1 jalapeño pepper, half chopped and half sliced
1 tablespoon fresh lime juice
5 tablespoons finely chopped bee balm leaves, plus small leaves
   for serving
1 large egg white
6 wheat (or rice) spring roll wrappers
1 cup rice vinegar
2 tablespoons sugar
1 teaspoon red pepper flakes
1 tablespoon cornstarch
Vegetable oil
6 Boston lettuce leaves

1. In a medium bowl, mix the crabmeat with the mayonnaise, chopped jalapeño, lime juice, and 3 tablespoons of the chopped bee balm.

2. Mix the egg white with 1 tablespoon water. Lay 1 spring roll wrapper flat, brush the edges with the egg white, and spread 3 tablespoons of the crab filling across the bottom of the wrapper. Roll it up, while folding in the sides like a burrito. When completely rolled, it should look like a tube sealed at both ends. Repeat with the remaining 5 wrappers and filling.

3. In a small saucepan over low heat, combine the sliced jalapeño, remaining 2 tablespoons chopped bee balm, the rice vinegar, sugar, and red pepper flakes. Mix the cornstarch with 1 tablespoon water and pour into the pan. Turn up the heat and simmer, stirring constantly, for a few minutes, or until thickened. Remove from the heat and pour into a small dipping bowl.

4. Pour ½ to 1 inch of oil into a frying pan and heat over high heat until a test bit of the wrapper dropped in the oil immediately sizzles. Fry the spring rolls in batches, turning until evenly golden brown, about 1 minute. Drain on paper towels to remove excess oil. Serve the spring rolls warm, wrapping each roll with some extra bee balm leaves and then a lettuce leaf before dipping into the sauce.

CHOKECHERRY *Prunus virginiana*

Foraging level: Yellow
Edible part: fruit only

This small tree is found in parks, wood edges, fields, and backyards throughout the United States and Canada (excluding the Southeast). The taste of the ripe cherry has a woodsy darkness to it that in my mind is a true taste of the wild. If you eat it raw, in fact, it is so tart and bitter that you may indeed "choke." But when you cook it to make jelly, coulis, or syrup, the taste transforms into a complex sweet-sour with a bitter ending note, an excellent pairing with a chalky-nutty flavored soft cheese such as Tomme Crayeuse, as recommended at a Murray's Cheese shop tasting in New York City. Like other cherries, the fruit is round with a single hard pit. The ⅓-inch fruit grows in long raceme drooping clusters at the ends of the branches. The toxic leaves are alternate–toothed and have no hair running down the underside of the spine. In the summer, we spend many days outdoors in the early-morning sun, enjoying the dappled light moving through the cherry tree branches. My daughters look forward to these unstructured days, picking and jellying chokecherries, and I hope that they will always have these memories to carry with them into the world.

LAVENDER BERGAMOT *Monarda fistulosa* (SEE PHOTOGRAPH PAGE 28)

Foraging level: Red

Form: Herb (leaves)

Found in: Sunny fields, dry edges, and wood clearings throughout the United States (excluding California and Florida).

Growth habit: Spreads slowly through rhizomes; medium height, upright in stands.

Key characteristics: Opposite leaves, square stem, herbal—not minty—aroma and taste, distinctive lavender-colored flowers.

Harvest tips: Pick the leaves when very young (even early in the spring) or pick the younger leaves on the side of the stems later and through the summer. If you have a meadow or field full of lavender bergamot, pick some wild leaves, but otherwise plant in a sunny area in your garden with some room to spread.

I like the spicy half clove taste—which is neither minty nor reminiscent of either lavender or bergamot—better than Eddy, who prefers the bee balm. Still, he agrees it is tasty, especially if infused or with fruit such as in white peach jam.

YUCCA *Yucca filamentosa*
Foraging level: Green

An herbaceous plant originating in the American desert but widely planted over much of the United States as a landscape specimen, yucca has 2-foot-long swordlike smooth green leaves and an even taller flower stalk with bell-like creamy white flowers. The inedible tuber is different from the Latin yuca or cassava shrub, *Manihot esculenta*, which is known for its delicious starchy tuber. For the American yucca, it is the cooked buds and flowers that have definite culinary potential. The buds have a green-pea taste; the flowers are a bit bitter but could go well in a sugary dish.

YUCCA POD

Lavender Bergamot Gelatin, Strawberries, and Mascarpone

The subtle herbal spice of the leaves rounds out the sweet flavors of the strawberries and mascarpone. ❧ **Serves 4**

⅓ cup sugar
1 tablespoon fresh lemon juice
3 tablespoons finely chopped lavender bergamot leaves
4 gelatin sheets or 2 teaspoons unflavored powdered gelatin
12 ounces (1 pint basket) fresh strawberries, hulled and sliced
1¼ cups (9.5 ounces) mascarpone cheese
½ cup heavy cream
1 teaspoon pure vanilla extract

1. In a small saucepan, boil 1¼ cups water with the sugar and lemon juice for about 3 minutes. Turn off the heat and add the lavender bergamot.

2. Meanwhile, soak the gelatin sheets in cold water to soften, about 1 minute. Drain well, squeezing out excess water. (If using powdered gelatin, drizzle in 1 cup cold water, let stand for several minutes to soften, and then heat on low until completely dissolved.) Add the softened gelatin to the hot lavender bergamot infusion, whisking until melted and combined. Transfer the mixture to the refrigerator to cool for 10 minutes, or until the mixture thickens but is not solidified.

3. Arrange the strawberry slices in 4 cocktail glasses or other serving dishes. Pour the cool liquid on top of the strawberries to coat them. Refrigerate for about 30 minutes, or until fully set.

4. In a mixer, whip the mascarpone, heavy cream, and vanilla until the mixture holds soft peaks. Spoon on top of the strawberries and gelatin and serve.

ANISE HYSSOP OR BLUE GIANT HYSSOP *Agastache foeniculum* (SEE PHOTOGRAPH PAGE 25)

Foraging level: Red

Form: Herb (leaves, flowers)

Found in: Gardens throughout the United States; in open sunny ground, dry fields, and thickets in the northern half of the United States. If you can't find it you can substitute *Hyssopus officinalis.*

Growth habit: Tall, slightly spreading.

Key characteristics: Leaves grow opposite along a square stem. Hyssop can get tall, even "giant," at 2 to 4 feet, towering over other mints; it has the smell of anise when the leaf or flower is crushed. The tubular flowers are bluish violet and are clustered together in aromatic spikes.

Harvest tips: Selectively pinch or clip off leaves or flowers from your meadow garden.

I will always remember this mint family herb, with the taste of summer anise, as the one that started this creative collaboration. The simplest way to enjoy it is by crushing a small leaf or dropping a lavender flower into a glass of Prosecco.

Anise Hyssop Gazpacho

Don't worry when this gazpacho is not a tomato red color—it more than makes up for it in flavor: sweet, salty, and with an unexpected hit of herbal anise. Serve garnished with ricotta or feta, if desired.

➴ **Serves 6**

16 ripe red plum tomatoes
1 ounce (25 large, 3- to 5-inch) anise hyssop leaves,
    plus small leaves for garnish
6 slices (6 ounces) white bread without the crust, torn into
    rough pieces
⅓ cup sherry vinegar
2 tablespoons extra-virgin olive oil
1 tablespoon sugar
1 teaspoon salt
1 teaspoon red pepper flakes

1. Bring a large saucepan of water to a boil. Have ready a bowl of ice water. Add half of the tomatoes to the boiling water and cook for 15 seconds to loosen the skins. Transfer to the ice water to cool. Repeat with the remaining tomatoes. Core and peel the tomatoes, then slice in half, removing any large clusters of seeds.

2. Transfer the tomatoes to a blender or food processor and add the anise hyssop, bread, vinegar, olive oil, sugar, salt, and red pepper flakes. Puree for a minute or more until smooth. Pour into a bowl and refrigerate for at least 30 minutes. Serve cold.

Anise Hyssop, Watermelon, and Parma Ham

The juicy, cold watermelon soaks up and intensifies the anise hyssop's unique flavor while the saltiness of the ham adds complexity.

🍵 **Serves 4 as an appetizer**

4 cups cubed seedless red watermelon
1 ounce (25 large, 3- to 5-inch) anise hyssop leaves
¼ cup extra-virgin olive oil
1 tablespoon white balsamic vinegar
½ teaspoon salt
10 drops Tabasco
6 thin slices Parma ham, prosciutto, bresaola, or other cured meat,
    torn into 2- to 3-inch pieces

1. In a blender or food processor, combine ½ cup of the watermelon, half of the anise hyssop leaves, the olive oil, vinegar, salt, and Tabasco and puree until smooth.

2. Arrange the remaining 3½ cups diced watermelon in plates or bowls and lightly spoon the dressing over the fruit. Roughly chop the remaining anise hyssop leaves and scatter them over the top along with the ham.

WILD MINTS WITH A MINTY TASTE: LAMIACEAE FAMILY

There are seemingly infinite kinds of mint growing wild around the world, many escaping the confines of their containers or garden beds and others starting off in the wild. Do not worry about distinguishing mints by identifying the species, particularly since we like to harvest them before they bloom, when it is even more difficult to tell the exact species or hybrid crossing of species. Mints in general are identifiable by the square stem, opposite leaves, and (usually) minty fragrance when crushed. Some mints are gentle and mellow, while others are hot and spicy, though the taste of one kind of mint can vary depending on the site and maturity. Sharper mints, such as peppermint [foraging level: Green] or the American mountain mints *Pycnanthemum* spp. [foraging level: Yellow], with a mint taste so strong you will fall off your chair, are better infused or in a jelly.

WILD SPEARMINT *Mentha spicata* (SEE PHOTOGRAPH PAGE 28)

Foraging level: Green	**Growth habit:** Spreads in stands through rhizomes; variable (sprawling, upright and becoming 2 feet tall)	odor (in contrast to a sharp, pepperminty odor).
Form: Herb (leaves, flowers)		**Harvest tips:** Pull out the plant or cut or pinch off upper stems with leaves. Wild mint leaves are tender and can brown easily, so store for a maximum of a few days in a plastic bag in the refrigerator without adding a moist paper towel.
Found in: Moist sunny areas, streambeds, and wet meadows throughout the United States and Canada (excluding North Dakota).	**Key characteristics:** Opposite leaves are attached to a square stem without a stalk. Leaves are hairless, crinkled, and toothed and have a spearminty aromatic	

After trying different wild mints, Eddy decided he prefers wild spearmint for its rounder, less sharp taste, which is more versatile for cooking. It is much better than commercially grown mints, which have a stiffer texture and less depth of flavor. As a substitute he also likes catnip (*Nepeta cataria*).

Lamb with Cucumber and Wild Spearmint

Spearmint pairs wonderfully with lamb, cucumber, and yogurt in this refreshing savory dish. ❧ **Serves 6**

³/₄ ounce (3 cups) wild spearmint leaves, plus more for serving
2 pounds lamb rib rack
3 tablespoons olive oil
Grated zest and juice of 1 lime
2 teaspoons red pepper flakes
1¹/₂ teaspoons salt
1 cup Greek yogurt
¹/₄ cup mayonnaise
1 tablespoon Dijon mustard
2 cucumbers, preferably seedless, peeled and sliced in long strips

1. Roughly chop 1 cup of the mint leaves. Marinate the lamb for a few hours in a bowl in the refrigerator in the chopped mint, olive oil, lime zest, half of the lime juice, half of the red pepper flakes, and 1 teaspoon of the salt.

2. Preheat the oven to 400°F.

3. In a medium bowl, mix the yogurt with the mayonnaise, mustard, remaining 1 teaspoon red pepper flakes, remaining 2 cups mint, and remaining ¹/₂ teaspoon salt. Stir in the cucumbers.

4. Put the lamb in a roasting pan and roast for 25 minutes, or until medium rare. Let rest for 10 minutes before slicing between the chops. Arrange the lamb on top of the cucumber salad, drizzle with the remaining lime juice and any pan juices, and garnish with mint leaves.

Chocolate-Dipped Wild Spearmint Leaves

These chocolate-covered mint leaves have a fresh, wild flavor that sets them apart from other chocolate-covered treats. Serve as an after-dinner refreshment with tea or coffee.

1. Lay a sheet of parchment paper on a baking sheet that will fit in your refrigerator. Melt 2 ounces good-quality bittersweet chocolate (60% cacao minimum; not chips) in a microwave or double boiler, stirring until smooth. Let cool until it is just warm when you dip a finger in it.

2. Holding the base of a mint leaf with your fingers (or blunt tweezers), dip each leaf into the melted chocolate, wipe off the excess chocolate on the side of the bowl or pot, and then place the leaf flat on the parchment paper. Continue dipping the leaves one by one. When finished, place the baking sheet in the refrigerator to set the chocolate.

3. Spoon unsweetened cocoa powder in the bottom of a small lidded container. Peel each leaf off the parchment paper, place in the container, and cover the leaf in the cocoa powder, adding more cocoa powder in layers as you fill the container. Keep the container in the refrigerator and take out the chilled chocolate leaves just before serving.

Wild Mint Green Tea with Toasted Pine Nuts

A Tunisian friend invited Eddy over for some afternoon mint tea with nuts and homemade pastries. He first thought that nuts in tea seemed "bizarre" but, after trying it, loved the way the sappy and minty flavors combine. ⊱ **Makes 5 cups tea**

1 bag green tea
3 ounces (3 to 4 cups) wild spearmint or catnip
¼ cup sugar
⅓ cup toasted pine nuts

1. In a large pot, bring 6 cups water to a boil. Place the tea bag in a large teapot and pour 1 cup boiling water over the bag. Let it infuse for 20 seconds, then discard (or drink!) the green tea water. This step tones down the strong flavor of the green tea. Leave the tea bag in the teapot.

2. Add the mint leaves, sugar, and remaining 5 cups boiling water to the teapot. Let infuse for at least 5 minutes. Strain the tea and serve warm or at room temperature in small glasses, adding pine nuts to each glass.

WILD ROSE *Rosa multiflora* (SEE PHOTOGRAPH PAGE 29)

Foraging level: Green

Form: Shrub (flowers)

Found in: Sunny hedgerows, thickets, edges of fields and forests throughout the eastern and central United States. In the western United States, substitute *Rosa californica* (foraging level: Yellow) and in the north, substitute *Rosa virginiana* (foraging level: Yellow), with lovely fragrant and larger pink flowers.

Growth habit: Invasive; coarse arching branches in thickets. Can grow to 10 feet tall and new plants can even form from where the canes touch the ground.

Key characteristics: With thorns that are curved and barblike, multiflora rose has smallish white flowers and a little beard fringe at the crook of the stem and the leaf. A single petal is shaped like a tiny heart.

Harvest tips: Cut off entire branches and bring them back or pluck off larger petals. Since the multiflora rose petals easily flutter off the stems, it is not so cumbersome to remove them as you might think. If you leave the clusters on the branches for a few hours in a brown paper bag, many of the petals will naturally fall off and gather at the bottom of the bag. You can also shake the remaining branches over the bag. (For the larger-petaled native wild roses [foraging level: Yellow], selectively pluck petals off individual flowers and you will soon gather a bagful.)

When the sweet, heady scent of the wild rose fills the hedgerows between the farm fields, I wander among the thickets and cut off large clusters of the rose, weighed down with flowers. Eddy is entranced with the floral scent escaping from the bag and filling the reception area of the restaurant.

Wild rose petals are much smaller and more delicate than the several-inch-wide garden roses we are used to. From a culinary point of view this enables them to be used whole, and without worrying about the bitter white pith that must be cut away when cooking with the usual garden roses.

Rose Petal Jam

This jam uses minimal cooking time to preserve the delicate texture and aroma of the rose petals. Our favorite way to enjoy this jam is to mix it with slivered almonds and a tablespoon of cornmeal to make a paste. We slather the paste on seared duck and serve extra on the side. The sweet floral taste of the wild rose petals is a perfect match for the fatty duck meat. ⌁ **Makes 3 cups**

> 2½ ounces (3 cups) wild rose petals (from 1 grocery bagful of
>   flower-laden branches)
> 1¾ cups sugar
> ¼ cup fresh lemon juice
> 1 (1¾-ounce) package powdered pectin
> 1 tablespoon rosewater (optional)

1. Set a small plate in the freezer for testing the jam later. In a large pot, bring 2 cups water to a boil. Add the rose petals, turn off the heat, cover, and steep for 30 minutes or more.

2. Turn the heat back on to high and bring to a boil, adding the sugar ½ cup at a time, waiting for it to boil after each addition. Add the lemon juice.

3. Put the pectin in a heat-safe 1-cup measure and vigorously mix in a small amount of the hot liquid so that the pectin does not become lumpy. Pour the dissolved pectin mixture back into the pot and rapidly boil on high heat, stirring continuously, for 2 minutes. Check the consistency by dropping a teaspoon of the hot jelly onto the chilled plate and leaving it in the freezer for 10 seconds. When you run a finger through the gel on the plate it should form a trail or otherwise achieve the consistency you are looking for. If it does not, continue to boil for 2 more minutes. Remove from the heat. If you prefer a stronger rose taste, add the rosewater. Pour into glass jars and refrigerate.

Rose Petal and Pistachio Raspberry Custard

Eddy was inspired by his Afghan mother-in-law's recipe for *firni*, traditionally a special-occasion milk pudding with pistachios and cardamom. The subtle rose flavors blend well in this only slightly sweet simple custard with green, red, and white colors. It can be made a day ahead and served at room temperature or slightly chilled. ❧ **Serves 6**

    1 quart whole milk
    4 ounces (5 cups) wild rose petals, plus more for decoration
       (from 2 grocery bagfuls of flower-laden branches)
    ¼ cup sugar
    1 teaspoon pure vanilla extract
    ½ cup cornstarch
    1 teaspoon rosewater, or to taste (optional)
    1 pint fresh raspberries
    2 tablespoons coarsely ground unsalted pistachios

1. In a large heavy saucepan, bring the milk almost to a boil, then remove from the heat. Remove ½ cup of the milk and set aside. Gently mix the rose petals into the warmed milk in the pan and let infuse for 15 to 20 minutes. Strain the milk through cheesecloth or a fine strainer, discarding the petals.

2. Pour the infused milk back into the saucepan, add the sugar and vanilla, and bring to a simmer over medium heat.

3. Whisk the cornstarch into the reserved ½ cup milk until there are no lumps. Add the cornstarch mixture to the pan and simmer over low heat, stirring gently with a rubber spatula, for 7 to 10 minutes, or until it is thickened and coats the spatula. Remove from the heat and let cool.

4. Eddy loves the subtle taste of the wild roses in this dish but if you prefer a stronger rose flavor, add the rosewater. Gently fold in the raspberries. Ladle into separate dessert dishes and sprinkle the top with ground pistachios. Cool in the refrigerator. Serve chilled or at room temperature.

YELLOW WOOD SORREL *Oxalis stricta*

(SEE PHOTOGRAPH PAGE 30)

Foraging level: Yellow

Form: Herb (leaves, flowers)

Found in: Sunny disturbed areas, garden beds, vegetable gardens, lawns, and edges throughout the United States and Canada (excluding California).

Growth habit: Spreads slowly through rhizomes; low (8 inches) to the ground.

Key characteristics: Three-part little heart-shaped leaflets look like a shamrock but not a clover, with small yellow flowers and a texture that is very soft and not stiff. The sour taste is due to the presence of oxalic acid, which in very large amounts may affect kidney functions and so should be eaten in moderation, as it has been by Indian tribes for centuries.

Harvest tips: Pinch off and keep the soft tips and leaves or pull out the plant and cut off the stiff parts.

This diminutive plant, found around the world, is sometimes also called "sour grass." After the yellow flowers bloom, it forms small conehead-shaped seed capsules that explode to throw the seed several feet away. Eddy likes the tender shape and taste of this common oxalis, and immediately puts it to use raw with lobster and peach.

Scallops and Wood Sorrel with White Wine Shallot Sauce

This dish has a beautiful light yellow color, and the tartness of the wood sorrel complements the scallops and shallots. ⤙ **Serves 4**

  3 small shallots, chopped
  1 cup dry white wine
  8 ounces (1 cup) crème fraîche
  1$\frac{1}{2}$ tablespoons unsalted butter
  10 large sea scallops, muscle removed, cut into $\frac{1}{2}$-inch pieces
  1 ounce (2$\frac{1}{4}$ cups) wood sorrel leaves
  $\frac{1}{2}$ teaspoon fresh lemon juice
  Salt and freshly ground black pepper

1. In a large shallow saucepan, cook the shallots and white wine over medium heat until the liquid reduces to about 2 tablespoons. Add the crème fraîche and simmer until the mixture reduces to about $\frac{1}{3}$ cup.

2. Heat a large skillet over medium-high heat. Add the butter and scallops and sear for 1 minute. Pour in the shallot sauce and add the wood sorrel. Cook for 30 seconds, stirring gently. Remove from the heat and season with the lemon juice and salt and pepper. Serve immediately.

PINEAPPLE WEED *Matricaria discoidea* (SEE PHOTOGRAPH PAGE 28)

Foraging level: Green

Form: Herb (flowers and leaves)

Found in: Open sunny gravel, such as driveway edges and flower and garden beds, throughout the United States (excluding Texas and Florida) and Canada.

Growth habit: Low growing, only a few inches to a foot high.

Key characteristics: It looks much like chamomile, with very fine lacy, fernlike dissected leaves and a yellow dome or cone that would be the middle of a flower, but with few or no white petals. Test by crushing the flowers and checking for a pineapple aroma.

Harvest tips: Cut the top 4 to 5 inches of the plant, flowers as well as leaves. Some plants in fertile soil conditions may grow taller and form petals; however, the flowers with petals appear to lose their pineappley aroma and should not be used.

I brought in a single plant to Eddy and he thought it looked a little bedraggled; I agreed that it looked like some petalless cousin of the chamomile. He did not have high hopes but was amazed that after being infused in hot water, it had a very aromatic herbal pineapple flavor with notes of chamomile.

HEAL ALL *Prunella vulgaris*
Foraging level: Yellow

This small herbaceous plant grows in sun and part shade in disturbed areas, gardens, lawns, and forest edges throughout much of the United States and Canada. It has the square stems and opposite oblong entire leaves common to the mint family, but no mint aroma. The small blue-violet hooded flowers bloom throughout the summer in a rectangular boxy shape on top of the low-growing stems. This shape earns it the Japanese name *utsubogusa*, for the boxy arrow quiver that samurai carry on their backs. It is most known for its holistic healing properties. We think the leaves and purple flowers taste spicy and herbal when young and become lemony sour when cooked. Substitute for galinsoga in Galinsoga and Ground Beef Polenta Pie (page 168).

Pineapple in Pineapple Weed Syrup

In this chilled dessert, the pineapple weed imparts a layered herbal complexity of pineappley flavor to the actual fruit. ❧ **Serves 4**

> ¼ **cup sugar**
> 1 **ounce (1 cup) pineapple weed leaves and flowers, plus more for garnish**
> 4 **fresh pineapple slices, quartered**
> 1 **pint vanilla ice cream or pineapple sorbet**

1. In a small saucepan, stir together 1¼ cups water and the sugar and bring to a boil over high heat. Add the pineapple weed and remove from the heat. Let infuse until cool. Strain, discarding the solids, and refrigerate until cold.

2. Divide the pineapple slices among individual bowls and spoon the chilled pineapple weed syrup on top so that it lightly surrounds the pineapple. In the center of each serving, add a scoop of vanilla ice cream. Garnish with a pineapple weed flower and a few small sprigs of leaves.

DAYLILY BUDS AND FLOWERS *Hemerocallis fulva*

(SEE PHOTOGRAPHS PAGE 26)

See Orange Daylily, page 82.

As summer arrives, the daylily shoots that introduced themselves in the spring have grown long and lanky and prelude the next act: the buds and flowers. The shoots grew stems about 3 feet high and each stem began to branch and form several buds, soft oblong tubes growing longer and turning from green to yellowish, ready to break open to a deep orange-red daylily, blooming for only a day. Then the next bud will take a turn so that the flowers twinkle on and off every day.

Harvest tips: Cut ripening stalks and wrap them in a bunch with a damp paper towel, then tightly bind the stalks together with plastic wrap, leaving the bottom of the bundle open, and place in a container filled with 5 inches of cool water. Keep upright at room temperature in indirect light until ready to use.

The buds have been used in Chinese cooking for over two thousand years and are known as "golden needles" (gold makes them lucky). The buds, a delicacy, are dried and shipped all over China. You might also recognize the buds as the oblong dried ingredients in a bowl of Chinese hot-and-sour soup or in the filling of moo shu pork.

Daylily Buds with Panko Bread Crumbs

When stir-fried, the buds taste wonderful, a little like asparagus but milder, juicier, softer—better. These go well with poached or steamed halibut or cod. ❧ **Serves 4**

>**3 tablespoons toasted sesame oil**
>**4 ounces (2 cups) 2- to 4-inch daylily buds**
>**1 teaspoon red pepper flakes**
>**Salt**
>**1/3 cup panko**
>**1/2 sheet nori (dried seaweed), torn into 1/2-inch pieces (optional)**

In a medium skillet over medium heat, heat the sesame oil. Add the daylily buds and red pepper flakes, season with salt, and cook, stirring occasionally, for 2 to 3 minutes, or until softened. Remove from the heat and stir in the panko and nori, if desired.

MULBERRY *Morus rubra*

Foraging level: Yellow

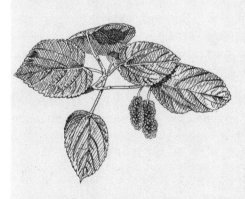

The mulberry tree is found naturally in the eastern and central United States but has also been planted extensively and hybridizes with the white mulberry, *Morus alba,* along forest edges, in farm fields, and in backyards. In early summer the slender dark red to black mulberry ripens, composed of many small berries together on a longish 1- to 2-inch cluster, like a curved pinky finger. Mulberries from red, white, and black mulberry trees cross with each other, and most of the common trees you see will be the Asian import, the white mulberry (don't go by the color of the berries, as they can still be red, but rather look at the lobed leaves of different shapes). Eddy adores the great flavor and juiciness of the fruit of the red mulberry tree, both tart and sweet, with a surprising Asian pear aftertaste. The white mulberry is not as tasty and almost bland in comparison. Mulberries can be a challenge to harvest as the trees can grow quite large and the birds can beat you to the berries.

Daylilies Stuffed with Lobster, Avocado, and Sushi Rice

This is Eddy's take on a stuffed zucchini flower—sushi style. The daylily holds its shape much better than a zucchini flower and of course the colors are gorgeously dramatic. Look for flowers that are about 4 inches long and no bigger so they wrap nicely over the stuffing.

❧ **Serves 4**

> **12 daylily flowers**
> **1/2 cup sushi rice**
> **2 tablespoons mirin**
> **2 tablespoons rice vinegar**
> **1 cup 1/2-inch chunks cooked lobster meat, king crab, or shrimp (12 chunks)**
> **1 Hass avocado, peeled, pitted, and cut into 12 chunks**
> **1/4 cup ponzu sauce (sold in the Asian section of grocery stores)**

1. Cut off each flower, leaving 1/4 inch of the stem attached. Pull out the pistils from the middle of the flowers and discard.

2. In a medium saucepan, combine the rice with 3/4 cup water and bring to a boil; then lower the heat and simmer, covered, for about 20 minutes, or until the water has evaporated and the rice is soft. Mix in the mirin and rice vinegar.

3. While the rice is still warm, using your hands, form 2 tablespoons of rice into an oblong about 1½ by 4 inches. On one side of the rice ball, press a chunk of lobster and on the other side, a chunk of avocado. Insert the oblong rice ball inside a flower and close the petals around the rice. Repeat with the remaining ingredients.

4. Serve the lilies on a plate, arranged in a circle around a small bowl of the ponzu sauce for dipping. They should be eaten within an hour.

WILD GARLIC HEADS *Allium vineale* (SEE PHOTOGRAPH PAGE 26)

See Wild Garlic, page 51.

Around the same time that the daylily flowers, another debutante from spring throws its hat on the stage. The wild garlic shoots will have grown a tall and wiry stem 2 to 4 feet high. The stem forms a little papery bulb at the end, shaped like a tiny white Christmas ornament. When it grows as large as your thumb, it splits open to reveal a marble-sized burgundy bumpy globe. Still later, the globe sprouts green shoots that grow upward, so that in the end the garlic head looks like someone who has had a fright with her hair standing on end.

Harvest tips: Cut the globes off at any time once they have split out from the paper covering and pull them apart. Scattered over the countertop will be numerous smooth teardrops the size of grains—these are the aerial bulblets of the wild garlic.

Eddy loves the shiny white bulblets tinged on one end in burgundy red, with a sweet garlicky taste and crunchy, juicy texture. Great to sprinkle on top of salads, in stir-fries, or over roasted meat.

MILE-A-MINUTE *Persicaria perfoliata*
Foraging level: Green

Also known as Asiatic tearthumb, this invasive vine is spreading north from the southern half of the United States in sunny areas over trees and small shrubs and has 1- to 2-millimeter backward (reflexed) barbs running down the vine, as well as on the underside of the perfectly triangular leaves. The tip of the leaf in contrast is smooth. It gets its name because it grows rapidly and can twine over and shade out trees and plants. After sautéing in butter until softened, the prickles disappear and it is quite fine to eat, with a bit of an acidic flavor reminiscent of sorrel. The biggest headache is to remove the leaves from the vine, because the entire stem of the vine is stiff and covered in prickles. But if you have a lot of them, you can substitute it for sorrel in Sheep Sorrel Risotto (page 99) or Scallops and Wood Sorrel with White Wine Shallot Sauce (page 155).

LAMBSQUARTERS *Chenopodium album* <small>(SEE PHOTOGRAPH PAGE 30)</small>

Foraging level: Green

Form: Herb (leaves)

Found in: Sunny disturbed ground—vegetable gardens, backyards, and tilled farm fields throughout the United States and Canada.

Growth habit: Found in groups, upright, reaching several feet tall.

Key characteristics: The linear alternate leaves are shaped like a rough diamond or even more like a goosefoot (translation of *Chenopodium*) and have a white powder on the underside. In fact, you can feel the powdery film on much of the smooth plant, and the leaves will repel water.

Harvest tips: Pinch or clip off the leafy tops of the young plant. On older plants that have not yet gone to seed, pinch off the younger offshoot branching sprigs that form on the sides of the main thick and tough stem.

Eddy recognizes this plant from France and finds that, when raw, the leaves taste like grass. But when tossed into an oiled pan or hot wok and flash-cooked, they have a nutty flavor that goes well with meats and fish. The texture becomes soft, like cooked spinach.

Curried Lamb and Lambsquarters Meatballs

Hurrah! Eddy dreamed up a ground meat recipe, one especially for meat lovers who may shy away when they see a lot of vegetables on their plate. The lambsquarters are mild and make the meatballs juicier. You can make these ahead of time and freeze them; defrost before frying. ❧ **Makes 15 large meatballs**

3 tablespoons olive oil
½ large onion, chopped
2 garlic cloves, chopped
4 ounces (4 cups packed) lambsquarters leaves
Salt and freshly ground black pepper
1 pound ground lamb or beef
1 heaping tablespoon curry powder
1 large egg yolk
Vegetable oil for frying

1. In a large skillet, heat the olive oil over medium heat. Sauté the onion and garlic for 3 minutes, or until softened. Increase the heat to high and add the lambsquarters and 1 teaspoon salt. Stirring occasionally, cook for 3 minutes, or until bright green and softened. Turn off the heat and let cool.

2. Meanwhile, in a large bowl, mix the ground meat with the curry powder and egg yolk. In a food processor, blend the lambsquarters mixture for 1 minute. Stir into the bowl with the ground meat. Mix well. It should look greenish. Using your hands, roll the mixture into 2-inch meatballs.

3. To cook the meatballs, pour ½ inch of vegetable oil into a large saucepan and heat over medium heat. Season the meatballs with salt and pepper and brown them well on both sides for 5 to 8 minutes, or until they become dark outside but are still a little pink inside. Test one to make sure it is not raw in the middle.

Lambsquarters Rigatoni Casserole

My youngest daughter's reaction when we were cooking this recipe together was: 1¼ cups of rigatoni is not going to be enough for me, Mom! But it turned out to be filling for four of us as a side dish with roast chicken. ❧ **Serves 4 as a side dish**

2 tablespoons unsalted butter, plus more for the dish
2 tablespoons olive oil
1¼ cups rigatoni
½ medium onion, chopped
6 ounces (6 cups packed) lambsquarters leaves
Salt
1 teaspoon ground nutmeg
1½ tablespoons all-purpose flour
1 cup heavy cream
2 large eggs
Tabasco
½ cup freshly grated Parmesan cheese

1. Preheat the oven to 400°F. Grease a 2-quart gratin dish.

2. Bring a large pot of salted water to a boil with the olive oil. Add the pasta and cook for about 10 minutes, or until al dente. Drain and transfer to the gratin dish.

3. In a large skillet, melt the butter over medium heat. Add the onion and cook for a few minutes or until softened, then add the lambsquarters, 1 tablespoon salt, and the nutmeg. Reduce the heat to low and cook for 2 minutes. Stir in the flour and heavy cream, turn the heat to high, and cook for 30 seconds, until almost boiling. Turn off the heat and let cool until warm.

4. In a food processor or blender, blend the lambsquarters mixture with the eggs until smooth. Season with salt and Tabasco. Pour the mixture evenly over the pasta and mix well. Top with the Parmesan cheese.

5. Bake for 2 to 5 minutes, or until the cheese has melted and the mixture is bubbling.

AMARANTH *Amaranthus retroflexus, Amaranthus hybridus*

(SEE PHOTOGRAPH PAGE 25)

Foraging level: Green

Form: Herb (young leaves, seeds)

Found in: Sunny farm fields and disturbed ground throughout the United States and Canada.

Growth habit: Weedy, aggressive, grows tall and straight.

Key characteristics: Amaranth looks like lambsquarters, with opposite leaves and a coarser, somewhat curved stem, but with no whitish film, which is characteristic of lambsquarters. Do not confuse the young plants with the toxic spiny horse nettle. Amaranth leaves are smooth all around with no lobes, and with no purplish tint on the undersides of the leaves. The *retroflexus* species that we use is also called red root amaranth, and the reddish root on the young plant makes it easier to identify.

Harvest tips: Choose green and tender plants up to 8 inches in height and cut or pinch off the leaves and young stems. On older plants that have not yet gone to seed, pinch off the younger tender offshoot leaves that form on the sides of the larger stalks.

Amaranth, or pigweed, is a very common farm field weed. But this plant has culinary roots, having come north to us from Central and South America, where it is known as being high in vitamins A and C, protein, and minerals, and is used mostly by grinding the seeds into flour. And indeed the seeds are prolific, generating possibly up to 100,000 a year for a single plant.

Neither Eddy nor I was particularly interested in grinding the seeds into flour (seems too much like a full-time job) and we didn't expect too much from the leaves of the young plants—6 inches or shorter. But, surprise again: The cooked leaves taste nice, almost like a mildish mustard.

Amaranth and Feta Phyllo Triangles

With more flavor than spinach triangles and packed with vitamins, these quickly became a hit in our house; we like this so much we double the recipe when we make it because no one can eat just one.

☙ **Serves 4; makes 8 triangles**

4 tablespoons (½ stick) unsalted butter
2 medium leeks, white and light green parts only, chopped
2 garlic cloves, chopped
4 ounces (2 cups packed) amaranth leaves, roughly chopped
1 to 1½ teaspoons red pepper flakes, to taste
Salt
4 ounces feta cheese, crumbled (1 cup)
2 large eggs
4 (16 x 12-inch) sheets frozen phyllo dough, defrosted
¼ cup freshly grated Parmesan cheese (optional)

1. Preheat the oven to 350°F.

2. In a large skillet, melt the butter. Pour off half of it and set aside. Add the leeks and garlic to the pan and cook over medium heat for 2 minutes. Add the amaranth, red pepper flakes, 2 generous pinches of salt, and ¼ cup water. Cook over low heat for 3 minutes, or until the liquid has evaporated. Remove from the heat and transfer to a medium bowl. Add the feta and eggs and mix to combine.

3. Lay one of the sheets of phyllo dough on a smooth work surface. Cut the sheet in half so it becomes an 8 × 12-inch rectangle. Lightly brush the top surface of the rectangle with the reserved melted butter, then fold it in half so it becomes a double-layered 4 × 12-inch sheet with the buttered parts on the inside. Divide the amaranth into 8 equal portions (about 3 tablespoons each). Place one portion on the bottom left corner of the phyllo, 1 inch from the end. Fold the corner up over the filling into a triangle shape. Press down to seal. Continue to fold up the sheet as you would fold a flag. Press the end to seal. Brush the top of the triangle with melted butter and sprinkle with grated Parmesan, if desired. Transfer to a baking sheet. Repeat with the remaining phyllo sheets.

4. Bake for 20 minutes, or until the edges are golden brown. Serve warm or let cool and then freeze. To reheat, defrost on the baking sheet and then bake.

GALLANT SOLDIERS *Galinsoga parviflora* and
SHAGGY SOLDIERS *Galinsoga ciliata* or *Galinsoga quadriradiata*

(SEE PHOTOGRAPH PAGE 27)

Foraging level: Green **Form:** Herb (young stems and leaves, small flowers) **Found in:** Sunny disturbed ground, farm fields, roadsides, and lawn edges throughout the United States and Canada (excluding Texas and the Southwest).	**Growth habit:** Aggressive weed, found in large numbers; seeds prolifically and may have several "seasons" of young plants in one calendar year. **Key characteristics:** Short plant; opposite hairy leaves and multiple branches with miniature daisylike flowers.	**Harvest tips:** Choose younger and leafier green tender plants and pinch off leaves and small flowers.

Galinsoga is named after a Spaniard, Mariano Martinez de Galinsoga, who first brought the plant from Peru to the Madrid Botanical Gardens. It is also known as quickweed because it germinates quickly and has rapidly spread from South and Central America to become one of the dominating agricultural weeds in the world. Traced to its roots in South America, galinsoga is cultivated for cooking and is known as *guascas* in the national Colombian Christmas soup, *ajiaco*, with chicken, corn, and potatoes. The young stems and leaves are also enjoyed in Southeast Asia. Eddy likes the mild taste, which is similar to that of peas and can mix well with lambsquarters.

Galinsoga and Ground Beef Polenta Pie

A simple, one-dish hearty meal with a lot of flavor, a bit in the style of a shepherd's pie (with no crust or gluten). ⌁ **Serves 6**

    1 cup polenta
    3 tablespoons olive oil, plus more for the dish
    ½ large onion, chopped
    2 garlic cloves, chopped
    6 ounces (6 cups) galinsoga leaves and young stems
    Salt
    1 pound ground beef or chicken
    1 tablespoon ground cumin or hot curry powder
    1 teaspoon red pepper flakes
    1 cup freshly grated Parmesan cheese

1. Cook the polenta according to package directions, stir well, and set aside.

2. Preheat the oven to 350°F. Grease a 2¾-quart oval baking dish with olive oil.

3. In a large skillet, heat the olive oil over medium heat. Add the onion and garlic and cook for 3 minutes, or until softened. Stir in the galinsoga and 1 teaspoon salt. Cook for about 3 minutes. Add the ground meat, and cook for 7 minutes, or until browned. Add the cumin and red pepper flakes.

4. Spread one-quarter of the cooked polenta on the bottom of the baking dish. Layer the galinsoga mixture on top and then cover evenly with the remaining polenta. Sprinkle with salt and the Parmesan cheese. Bake for 15 minutes.

5. Increase the oven temperature to 500°F and bake for 5 minutes, or until the cheese is lightly browned and melted.

Galinsoga à la Crème

A hearty dish with crunchy croutons balancing the creaminess of the sautéed galinsoga. ❧ **Serves 4**

6 tablespoons (³/₄ stick) unsalted butter
¹/₂ cup cubed white bread (crusts removed)
4 ounces (4 cups) galinsoga leaves and young stems
2 tablespoons all-purpose flour
³/₄ cup whole milk
1 teaspoon ground nutmeg
1 tablespoon fresh lemon juice
Salt
Cayenne pepper

1. In a large skillet, melt 2 tablespoons of the butter over medium-high heat. Add the bread and toast for 2 to 3 minutes, or until golden brown. Transfer to a plate.

2. In the same pan, melt the remaining 4 tablespoons butter over medium heat. Add the galinsoga and sauté for about 4 minutes, until tender. Stir in the flour and then the milk and cook, stirring, over low heat for 2 minutes, until creamy.

3. Season with the nutmeg, lemon juice, and salt and cayenne to taste. Top with the crispy bread cubes.

SHISO *Perilla frutescens* (SEE PHOTOGRAPH PAGE 29)

Foraging level: Green **Form:** Herb (leaves, seeds) **Found in:** Fields, edges of fields, and garden beds (from which it often escapes) in the eastern and central United States.	**Growth habit:** Aggressive, can be invasive; grows upright in groups, and can become several feet high. **Key characteristics:** Square stem, opposite fan-shaped leaves with heavily toothed and frilly edges. Very aromatic.	**Harvest tips:** Pluck off the smaller tender leaves. Use precautions not to spread the seeds, which are also great to eat.

If you have ever eaten a leaf wrapped around your sushi or sashimi, you have probably already eaten shiso, the heavily perfumed Asian herb. It became a trendy gourmet ingredient some years back and I have occasionally seen it carefully stacked in plastic-wrapped packages in high-end grocery stores. Shiso has escaped from gardens and is now quickly spreading. The fresh wild version is an ocean apart from the stiff, flavor-depleted stack of leaves you can find in gourmet grocers.

Eddy likes the local and wild version better than the prepackaged leaves. The complex, aggressive flavor is difficult to describe—something like cilantro with lemony and basil notes. It has a soft and frilly texture that is quite nice in salads, tempura, and tucked into summer rolls.

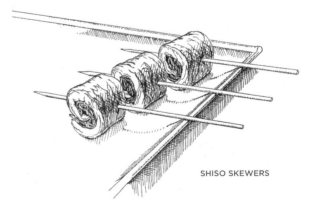

SHISO SKEWERS

Shiso Beef Tenderloin Skewers

These are loaded with flavor, have a nice pinwheel shape, and are great for summer grilling. If using wooden skewers, soak them in water for 30 minutes to prevent burning. ❧ **Serves 4**

    1 pound beef tenderloin
    Salt
    1 teaspoon red pepper flakes
    20 medium to large shiso leaves
    1 cup teriyaki sauce

1. Slice the tenderloin in half horizontally so that you have 2 thin steaks (ideally about ¼ inch thick), each about 9 by 4 inches. Pound the meat with a meat pounder to even out the thickness and shape. Season each steak with salt and red pepper flakes and cover the top of each steak with 10 shiso leaves, overlapping them to fit.

2. On a large baking sheet, with the long side facing you, tightly roll the meat with the shiso inside to form 2 long horizontal cylinders. Then insert the skewers working from one side of the cylinder to the other every ¾ inch along each cylinder so that each roll holds its shape. Carefully slice cleanly through the meat roll in between each skewer to make several skewered pieces per roll. Turn each skewer flat so you can see the cross section of the roll. Spoon the teriyaki sauce evenly over the skewered meat rolls and let marinate for a few hours in the refrigerator.

3. Heat a grill to high or preheat the broiler.

4. Grill the beef, turning once, for about 8 minutes, or until medium rare.

Shiso Tabbouleh with Cucumber, Avocado, Tomato, and Tofu

This is a raw salad—though at first I made the mistake of just reading the couscous package and cooking the couscous, and the dish turned out mushy, much to Eddy's dismay. In fact, the uncooked couscous absorbs the lemon juice and olive oil and becomes fluffy and light. The shiso gives a flavor boost to this healthy addition to a summer picnic or barbecue. ✺ **Serves 8**

1 cucumber
8 ounces (2 cups) couscous
1 (10-ounce) package firm tofu, drained and diced
4 medium tomatoes, diced
1 medium red onion, diced
1 Hass avocado, peeled, seeded, and cubed
20 medium to large shiso leaves, coarsely chopped, plus small leaves
    for garnish
¾ cup fresh lemon juice
¾ cup extra-virgin olive oil
1 teaspoon red pepper flakes, or to taste
2 teaspoons salt, or to taste

1. Peel and halve the cucumber. In a blender, puree one half with ¼ cup water until smooth. Dice the remaining half.

2. In a large bowl, combine the diced and pureed cucumber, the couscous, tofu, tomatoes, onion, avocado, shiso, lemon juice, olive oil, red pepper flakes, and salt. Gently toss and let rest in the refrigerator for about 1 hour before serving. Garnish with small shiso leaves.

WILD BLUEBERRY *Vaccinium* spp. (SEE PHOTOGRAPH PAGE 29)

Foraging level: Yellow

Form: Shrub (berries)

Found in: Acidic soils in forests, mountains, bogs, thickets, and even northern lawns; grows naturally in the northern half of the United States but also found as far south as Georgia as well as at farmer's markets and local festivals.

Growth habit: Highbush blueberry is upright and can reach 10 feet; lowbush blueberry hugs 1 foot to the ground. Both species can form dense thickets.

Key characteristics: Bluish to blackish fruit sometimes has a white "bloom" on the surface. The fruit is round and has a five-part crown shape on one end. The branches have no thorns.

Harvest tips: Cover up against the mosquitoes and no-see-ums, and wear a hat and boots. Strap an open container to your waist to pick the berries.

The wild blueberry is smaller and less juicy than the commercially farmed blueberry, but its taste is more deep and flavorful. Lovely in desserts, the wild blueberry's flavor can also pair well with savory dishes and meats.

FORAGER'S JOURNAL

Berry picking with a bucket or sawed-off milk carton tied around your waist, hands free, is a summer tradition. So if wild blueberries, huckleberries, raspberries, juneberries, and blackberries are plentiful in your neck of the woods, enjoy them using a foraging level–Yellow approach, picking only a limited percentage or planting some local species. These berries can be used interchangeably in the mixed-berry recipes. Avoid round red berries or berries on vines as some of these are poisonous or toxic.

Wild Berry Panna Cotta

This tastes like a less rich and sweet version of a berry cheesecake and is lovely to serve at a dinner party in individual cups. You can make it up to a day ahead and refrigerate it until ready to serve.

 Serves 6 to 8

14 ounces (3 cups) mixed wild berries
2 tablespoons blackberry or raspberry jam
4 gelatin sheets or 2 teaspoons unflavored powdered gelatin
1 pound mascarpone cheese
1 cup milk
1/3 cup sugar
1 teaspoon pure vanilla extract

1. In a medium bowl, mix the berries and the jam with a fork, roughly crushing the berries.

2. Soften the gelatin sheets in cold water for 1 minute, then drain well and squeeze out the excess water with your hands. (If using powdered gelatin, add 1 cup water, let stand for several minutes to soften, and then heat on low until completely dissolved.)

3. In a saucepan, bring the mascarpone, milk, sugar, and vanilla just to a boil over medium-high heat. Remove from the heat, add the softened gelatin, and whisk to combine. Cool in the refrigerator for 5 to 10 minutes, or until the mixture is just starting to gel but is still loose.

4. Spoon the crushed berries equally into glasses or ramekins until halfway full, smoothing the tops. Pour the mascarpone mixture over the berries and refrigerate for 1 to 2 hours, or until set, before serving.

Wild Berry Popsicles

The rich and layered blend of wild berry tastes makes this an out-of-the-ordinary treat. If you don't have Popsicle molds, this also makes for a great sorbet. ❧ **Makes 14 popsicles**

1 cup sugar
¹⁄₂ teaspoon pure vanilla extract
14 ounces (3 cups) mixed wild berries

1. In a medium saucepan, bring 2 cups water, the sugar, and vanilla to a boil. Remove from the heat.

2. In a blender, puree the berries and then pour in the sugar syrup. Blend continuously for about 2 minutes, or until completely smooth. Pass through a fine-meshed strainer or several layers of cheesecloth, discarding the solids. Spoon into molds and freeze for at least 4 hours, until solid.

WINEBERRY *Rubus phoenicolasius*

Foraging level: Green

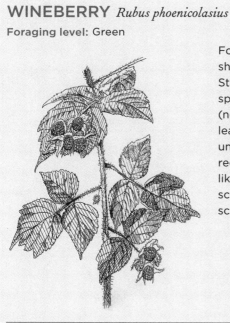

Found in open woods, wood edges, and disturbed part-shade areas throughout the eastern and central United States, this invasive plant grows in arching canes, spreading in thickets. The cane has very, very fuzzy (not thorny) reddish hairs all over. The heart-shaped leaves group themselves in threes and have silvery undersides. The fruit looks like a more intense scarlet-red version of a raspberry; it is juicy and sweet, tasting like a red currant. Eddy turns the ripe red berries into a scarlet-colored jelly to serve with yogurt, waffles, and scones.

PURSLANE *Portulaca oleracea* (SEE PHOTOGRAPH PAGE 30)

Foraging level: Green

Form: Herb (leaves and flowers)

Found in: Sunny open disturbed ground near the house, vegetable and garden beds, and farm fields throughout the United States and Canada and much of the temperate world.

Growth habit: Low, sprawling.

Key characteristics: Sprawling, fleshy, succulent, almost cactus-looking little $1/2$- to 1-inch oval pads (without the thorns); yellow flowers and tiny black seeds (no, those are not bugs).

Harvest tips: Cut the end tips off the main stems, which grow thicker and coarser as the plant matures. If you keep cutting the tips back while they are young, tender, glossy, and crisp, they continue to grow back all summer, like "cut and come again" lettuces.

Purslane is one of Persia's lasting gifts to the world, lauded as one of the highest natural sources of omega-3 and now found in many farmer's markets. Eddy is very familiar with purslane, known as *pourpier* in France. It has a mild, somewhat lemony taste and a succulent texture.

176 | FORAGED FLAVOR

Purslane, Artichoke, Manouri Cheese, and Black Olive Salad

Raw sliced artichokes, a salad fixture in the South of France, have enough texture to stand up to the crunchy purslane. The black olives and cheese add saltiness and depth of flavor. ❧ **Serves 4**

2 lemons
8 to 10 baby artichokes
6 ounces (4 cups) tender purslane tips and small leaves
¼ cup pitted brined black olives, drained
5 ounces manouri or feta cheese, cut into small cubes (1¼ cups)
⅓ cup extra-virgin olive oil
1 to 2 teaspoons cayenne pepper, to taste

1. In a medium bowl of water, squeeze the juice from one of the lemons. Prepare the artichokes one by one: Discard the darker green outer leaves; leave the inner yellow leaves that are slightly moist and tender. Holding the artichoke stem side up, with a paring knife, peel the outer layer from the stem. Cut off the bottom inch of the stem and then cut off the tops of the leaves to remove any slightly greener parts and the pointy tips. Transfer to the lemon water while preparing the remaining artichokes.

2. When ready to serve, thinly slice the artichokes lengthwise and toss into a large bowl. Add the purslane, olives, cheese, and olive oil. Squeeze the juice from the remaining lemon into the bowl and season with cayenne.

Purslane Eggplant Caponata

The eggplants and onion smell wonderful cooking on the stove, and the purslane takes on an almost nutty flavor with a little heat from the cayenne pepper. This goes very nicely with sausages. ❧ **Serves 6**

¼ cup olive oil
2 small to medium (12 ounces) thin eggplants, cut into ¼- to ½-inch dice
1 medium red onion, cut into ½-inch dice
2 tablespoons honey
2 teaspoons salt
2 teaspoons cayenne pepper
6 ounces (4 cups) tender purslane tips and small leaves, plus more for serving
2 tomatoes, diced
¼ cup toasted pine nuts
½ cup balsamic vinegar

In a medium skillet over medium heat, heat the olive oil and add the eggplants. Cook, stirring occasionally, for 2 to 3 minutes, until softened. Add the onion, honey, salt, and cayenne. Reduce the heat to low and add the purslane, tomatoes, pine nuts, and vinegar. Simmer for 2 to 3 minutes, or until it reaches the consistency of a stew. Decorate with fresh purslane.

ORACHE *Atriplex hortensis*

Foraging level: Yellow

Also known as French spinach or salty lambsquarters, orache can be found growing on sand and seashores throughout much of the United States and Canada (excluding the Southeast), both sprawling and erect, reaching 2 to 5 feet high with smooth goosefoot-shaped leaves that are mostly toothed but sometimes not. It looks very similar to lambsquarters but without the whitish bloom. We prefer it cooked, not raw, and the chefs swooned over the taste with its briny highlights and the soft texture when sautéed with a bit of olive oil. In harvesting, exercise caution regarding the quality of the surrounding environment and waters.

AUTUMN
& WINTER

AUTUMN

WINTER

When the lawn grass has withered and turned brown and landscapers are shutting down for the season, wild autumn is exploding with color and energy: Vibrant flowers illuminate the meadows like sparklers, seeds change their shapes ready to scatter to the wind or hitch a ride, and fruits and nuts ripen and bulge. Birds are migrating, animals and insects are storing up before winter, things are on the move. The colors change from green to orange, yellow, red, sienna, glossy black. When Eddy thinks of the taste of autumn he thinks of mushrooms from the moist, dark earth; nuts and fruits from the forest trees; and the last burst of greens before a hard frost.

Foraging is plentiful right through December and it's a delight to wander about through crisp-cool azure days. A number of the early spring plants do double duty in the fall, so please accept their overtime work and enjoy more meals: wild garlic, cardamine, chickweed, garlic mustard, artemisia, deadnettle, ground ivy, and creeping jenny are all up and about, although slowly fading as the days grow colder.

Winter for foragers really only begins once the snow blankets the ground or the temperature drops below 20°F. I enjoy the stillness of the nights and mornings, my breath frosty in the air, the crunch of frozen ground under my boots, the hues of chocolate brown, ivory, and gray making a beautiful palette in the wild. This is when Eddy starts to seriously pester me about finding things for him: "What about sticks and bark?" he asks. Actually, not a bad idea . . .

FORAGER'S JOURNAL

Fruit and seed production often goes in cycles. Some years there is a glut of a fruit, due to optimal weather conditions or the natural rhythm known as a mast year for trees. We appreciate our wild bounty even more now that we realize that this autumn's plentiful beechnut harvest may not return for another three to five years. Similarly, If there are poor conditions, the tree will conserve its resources and produce little if any fruit. This is a normal variability for wild fruits.

AUTUMN

QUEEN ANNE'S LACE *Daucus carota* (SEE PHOTOGRAPH PAGE 32)

Foraging level: Green

Form: Herb (fruits)

Found in: Sunny disturbed ground, lawns, roadsides, and fields throughout the United States and Canada.

Growth habit: Tall (2 to 3 feet high), straight, taproot.

Key characteristics: Flowers have 2- to 6-inch lacy white flower umbels (a shape like an umbrella); each usually has a little dark dot in the center. Oblong fruits framed by little fluttery eyelashes are inside the closed-up umbels, which look like bird's nests just turning brown.

Harvest tips: Timing is important. Select and cut off flower umbels that have folded up into the shape of a tiny bird's nest but have not yet gone completely brown. Smell inside the nest for a spicy aroma and examine closely so you can see that the green or reddish fruits have formed. You can keep the umbels at room temperature in a brown paper bag for a few days before opening the umbels, washing and removing the fruits and spreading them out on a baking sheet to dry for 10 minutes or longer.

This old-fashioned European plant is the ancestor of today's cultivated carrot. I bring Eddy a couple of flower clusters. He sniffs the flower (there is no smell) and I say, with somewhat forced enthusiasm, "This is Queen Anne's lace!" He looks at me quizzically and shrugs, not very interested. Then I find out from a friend in Paris that the French call this plant *carotte sauvage* and that the true culinary treasure is the fruit. I tromp around random fields and find that, sure enough, the little bird's nests that I always dismissed as a bunch of dead weeds contain fruits that are first green but become reddish and only later turn brown. When ripe, the fruits exude an intense spicy carrot aroma. I excitedly send Eddy a message: "How about *la carotte sauvage*?" "Ah! *La carotte sauvage*! Yes, very interested."

Eddy pan-fries the fruits in a little oil to bring out the flavor. He serves them atop a white fish with a dense carrot sauce and garnish. The wild carrot seeds give it an amazing kick, almost like coriander but with an intense essence of carrot.

CARROT FAMILY CAUTION: Many guidebooks warn against cooking with Queen Anne's lace unless you are sure of your botany. This has nothing to do with the plant itself but with its membership in the carrot family. There are many similar-looking species in this plant family, mainly known for its long taproots, finely divided leaves, and lacy umbels of yellow or white flowers. The family houses two of the most poisonous plants in North America: poison hemlock (*Conium maculatum*) and fool's parsley (*Aethusa cynapium*). So if you see a plant with white umbel flowers, be sure of your identification before venturing to shake hands. A number of culinary carrot family plants, such as wild chervil/honewort (*Cryptotaenia canadensis*) or the flowers of the Golden Alexander (*Zizia aurea*) or even the non-carrot-family yarrow (*Achillea millefolium*), are tasty but are not for everyday foraging because of the risk of misidentification. The beauty of using Queen Anne's lace fruit *only* is that poison hemlock seeds are found in a smooth green sack and are *not* curled up inside a little bird's nest, smelling like wild carrot, which makes the edible fruit easier to identify.

FORAGER'S JOURNAL

It's the dead of winter and there is a foot of snow on the ground. Hmm . . . how about trying sassafras twigs (as opposed to the roots, which are buried in the frozen ground)? They are aromatic and, of course, the basis for old-fashioned root beer.

Eddy has never heard of root beer so I bring in a bottle along with the cinnamon-colored sassafras twigs. I find Gregory, the executive sous chef, in the kitchen. He frowns. "Tama, I cannot have beer during working hours." I laugh, explaining that it is not really "beer" and does not contain alcohol. Eddy and Gregory inspect the bottle label: "But it says "root *beer*," they say. Gregory opens the bottle with anticipation; they sample it and then frown in disappointment: "Tastes like Coca-Cola." Eddy breaks a sassafras twig in half and sniffs the aroma. It is interesting; Gregory nods in agreement. Turns out it is actually more aromatic when simply infused in a hot liquid instead of simmered, which mutes the flavor. It does have a somewhat interesting aftertaste, a lingering spearminty, aromatic tinge of wintergreen.

Carrot Salad with Wild Carrot Fruits and Pickled Ginger

While I don't usually expect too much from a raw carrot salad, this is a surprisingly exciting dish with lime, pickled ginger, and mustard for a feast of flavors. ❧ **Serves 4 to 6**

1/3 cup orange juice
1/3 cup carrot juice
Juice of 1 lime
1/2 teaspoon salt
1/2 teaspoon cayenne pepper or harissa paste
1 tablespoon Dijon mustard
1/3 cup extra-virgin olive oil
8 to 10 medium carrots, peeled and then cut into long thin strips
    with a vegetable peeler or mandoline (7 cups)
1/3 cup wild carrot fruits (from 8 to 10 bird's nest clusters)
1 tablespoon pickled ginger (available at the grocery store
    sushi counter)

1. In a small pot, simmer the orange and carrot juices over medium heat for about 15 minutes, or until the liquid reduces to about 1/4 cup. Pour into a food processor or blender, add the lime juice, salt, cayenne, mustard, and oil, and blend thoroughly to make a smooth vinaigrette.

2. Toss the carrot strips, wild carrot fruits, and ginger with the vinaigrette. Serve.

Chocolate Mousse
with Wild Carrot Fruits

The intense wild carrot flavor pairs well with sweet as well as savory. Here Eddy makes a wild carrot "brittle" topping for chocolate mousse. It tastes crumbly, carrot-like, and gingerbready on top of the smooth creamy chocolate. Note that this mousse contains raw egg; use pasteurized eggs if you have concerns. ❧ **Serves 4 to 6**

1½ cups heavy cream
8 ounces dark chocolate (at least 70% cacao), broken into small pieces
4 tablespoons (½ stick) unsalted butter, softened
3 large eggs
½ cup plus 2 tablespoons sugar
1 teaspoon grapeseed oil
⅓ cup fresh wild carrot fruits or
  2 heaping teaspoons dried and ground

1. In a small saucepan, bring the heavy cream almost to a boil.

2. Meanwhile, in a medium heatproof bowl set over boiling water, melt the chocolate with the butter. Remove from the heat, add the hot cream, and whisk for 2 to 3 minutes until smooth. Set aside to cool to room temperature.

3. In a mixer, beat the egg whites with 2 tablespoons of the sugar until they form stiff peaks. Add the yolks and continue to whisk for a few seconds. Gently fold in the room-temperature (not hot) chocolate mixture.

4. Fill 4 to 6 individual ramekins with the mousse and refrigerate for at least 2 hours to set. If you like a really stiff mousse, leave it in the refrigerator overnight.

5. An hour or two before you are ready to serve, brush a sheet of parchment paper with the oil. In a medium saucepan over low heat, mix the remaining ½ cup sugar and ⅓ cup water and stir continuously for 5 to 7 minutes, until golden. Add the wild carrot fruits and continue to cook for 1 to 2 minutes. Test for doneness by adding a drop to a small cup of cold water. It should immediately harden like a candy.

6. Pour the mixture out onto the prepared parchment paper and let cool for 20 minutes until hardened. In a food processor, pulse the caramelized wild carrot coarsely. Spoon on top of the mousse.

SUMAC *Rhus* spp. (SEE PHOTOGRAPH PAGE 32)

Foraging level: Yellow

Form: Shrub or small tree (fruit clusters)

Found in: Hedgerows, road edges, and field edges with sun or partial shade throughout the United States.

Growth habit: Clonal stands grow 3 to 15 feet high.

Key characteristics: Upright, deep red torchlike fruit clusters.

Harvest tips: Find a tree with berries at their peak, when they are a glowing red and not brown. The berries lose their flavor as the clusters turn brown or begin to dry, as well as sometimes after heavy rains. Test by rubbing your finger on a berry to taste the tartness. Cut off a cluster where it ends on the branch. You can store clusters for a few days in a paper bag in a cool dark place. When ready to prepare, remove any clusters or parts of clusters that look grayish or mildewed and immerse the berries in cold, clean water, breaking apart the clusters so that individual berries can soak and be washed. If left to soak, the water will turn more red as the tart flavor infuses and becomes ready for jelly. Do not overly wash the clusters as this can rinse away some of the flavor.

Daniel and Eddy have been cooking with the European sumac *Rhus coriaria* for years. In Paris farmer's markets, sumac spice is a familiar sight, ground and dried in heaping piles. In Middle Eastern cuisine, sumac bestows a lemony taste to rice and meats. The American sumacs taste similar, but their color is much more beautiful, a deep red jewel-like flame, rather than the purple-brown of their European cousins.

When I first brought one of the deep red berry clusters to Eddy, he immediately exclaimed "sumac!" with surprise. He did not know it grew wild in the United States. "Can you bring me some more, Tama?" So the next week I brought in more. Eddy held up one of the sumac clusters to Daniel and said, with pride, "This is the American sumac!" Then I was asked to explain what it was and how it tastes: clean, tart, and dry—very refreshing.

Everyone passed the sumac around, feeling its rough texture, the tiny hairs and woody twigs. The smell was faintly tart but also sweet and earthy. A distinguished-looking gentleman in a double-breasted suit who had been talking to Daniel in the kitchen exclaimed excitedly, "I've seen that. I have that in my backyard! Never knew you could eat it."

Sumac-Ade

This drink is a not-too-sweet true thirst quencher and makes the most of the clean, dry character of the sumac berries. ❧ **Makes 2 quarts**

8 sumac berry clusters
Sugar, maple syrup, honey, or other sweetener

Immerse the sumac in 2 quarts cold water for a few hours. The water should turn a jewel-like red. Strain through a fine jelly cloth or several layers of cheesecloth to remove any twigs or fine hairs. Sweeten to taste. Serve chilled.

SUMAC VARIETIES

Smooth sumac, *Rhus glabra,* grows throughout the United States, and staghorn sumac, in the East. They taste the same but you may need one and a half times the volume of smooth (as opposed to staghorn) to achieve the same results. Staghorn sumac has fuzzy hairs all over the berries and branches, looking somewhat like the young velvety fuzzy antlers of a stag. You won't confuse these edible sumacs with poison sumac, *Toxicodendron vernix*, which has small white berries in loose clusters and tends to grow in wetter areas.

Sumac Jelly

Skip the canned cranberry sauce this autumn in favor of this tart and refreshing red jewel-colored jelly. Serve as an accompaniment to roast turkey and as a spread on turkey sandwiches the next day. Pascal Vittu, cheese steward for the restaurant, also recommends these cheese pairings: La Tur, a creamy blend of cow, goat, and sheep cheese; Red Cloud Colorado Haystack Mountain, a goat's-milk cheese; and an aged Cheddar such as Cabot Clothbound Cheddar or Julianna from Capriole Farm in Indiana. ❧ **Makes 3 cups**

8 to 10 clusters sumac berries
2 cups sugar
1 (1³/₄-ounce) box powdered pectin

1. Set a small plate in the freezer for testing the jam later. Loosen the sumac berries from their bunches and soak in 2 cups water for about 4 hours. The water should turn pink-red and taste tart. Strain the liquid through a jelly bag or several layers of cheesecloth. Pour the liquid into a medium pot and bring to a boil over high heat. Add the sugar ½ cup at a time, returning to a boil after each addition.

2. In a heat-safe 1-cup measure, vigorously mix the pectin with ¼ cup of the hot liquid so that the pectin does not become lumpy. Add the pectin mixture to the pot and boil for 3 minutes. Check the consistency by dropping a teaspoon of the hot jelly onto the chilled plate and leaving it in the freezer for 10 seconds. When you run a finger through the gel on the plate it should form a trail or otherwise achieve the consistency you are looking for. If it does not, continue to boil for 2 more minutes. Remove from the heat. Pour into glass jars and refrigerate.

Dried Sumac Spice

This is a pantry staple that can be made at the peak of sumac season and used throughout the year. Eight to ten sumac berry clusters will yield about 2½ cups spice.

Heat the oven to the lowest setting. After breaking apart the clusters and removing the twiggy core at the center, wash the sumac berries in cold water. (The water will turn pink and can be saved and strained for Sumac-Ade, page 191, and Sumac Jelly, page 192.) Spread the berries on a baking sheet lined with parchment paper and place them in the warm oven for about 3 hours until dry. Grind in a coffee or spice grinder. Sieve the powder to remove the larger seeds. Store the powder in an airtight container.

CHICKEN OF THE WOODS MUSHROOM *Laetiporus sulphureus*

Foraging level: Yellow

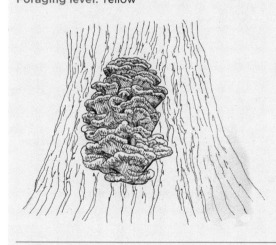

This mushroom, found throughout the temperate world, grows to a 12-inch or more heavy "shelf" on certain trees, such as oaks; it tastes best when bright yellow to orange. Its name alludes to its meaty texture when cooked. To harvest, cut with a knife, leaving 2 inches attached to the tree. Eddy sautées small mushroom chunks with butter, shallots, and a cream reduction before mixing them with braised wild greens, capturing the hearty essence of autumn.

Za'atar Spice

Many Middle Eastern families have their own secret recipe for za'atar, a spice blend chiefly used in cooking with meats and kebabs, soups and stews. The taste is nutty, subtly tart, and thoroughly Mediterranean. ⌣

Makes 1½ cups

> ½ **cup Dried Sumac Spice (page 193)**
> ½ **cup dried thyme, ground in a spice or coffee grinder**
> ½ **cup toasted sesame seeds**

Mix together the sumac, thyme, and sesame seeds and store in an airtight container for up to a year.

OYSTER MUSHROOM *Pleurotus ostreatus*

Foraging level: Yellow

These whitish gray stemless mushrooms, with gills on their undersides, commonly grow on downed tree logs and dead standing trees and can also be found in farmer's markets. In the wild, I see their size range from 2 inches to 8 inches. Their color and delicate faint seafood aroma explain their name. Oyster mushrooms seem like they throw a little party in the autumn after a rain. They should be harvested while still moist and flexible, not stiff or flabby. Cut the mushroom with a knife from the side of the log or tree, leaving an inch or so remaining on the tree. Place in a paper bag. They can be prepared in many ways, but we like them sautéed with butter and shallots or in a creamy stew or light curry.

Fried Chicken with Za'atar

These chicken nuggets are crisp and dry, as opposed to greasy, with a subtle blend of flavors. If you want more heat, add Korean or spicy pepper powder. ♨ **Serves 4**

> **2 cups plain yogurt**
> **4 tablespoons Za'atar Spice (preceding recipe)**
> **Salt**
> **2 teaspoons red pepper flakes**
> **Grated zest and juice of 1 lemon**
> **10 to 16 ounces boneless skinless chicken breast halves,**
>   **cut into 2- to 3-inch chunks**
> **Vegetable oil for frying**
> **2 cups all-purpose flour**
> **1 cup cornstarch**

1. Mix the yogurt with 2 tablespoons of the za'atar, 2 teaspoons salt, the red pepper flakes, and the lemon zest and juice. Rub the chicken pieces with the mixture and marinate overnight in the refrigerator.

2. In a medium skillet, pour in oil to a depth of 1 inch and heat over high heat. Mix the flour and cornstarch together. Coat the chicken pieces with the flour mixture, shaking off the excess. Test the temperature by dropping a piece of chicken into the oil. It should sizzle. Fry the chicken in batches, turning once, for about 4 minutes, or until golden. Remove and drain on paper towels. Season with salt and the remaining 2 tablespoons za'atar. Serve hot.

Sumac and Fig Tart

The tartness of sumac pairs well with sweet figs, which are in season around the same time. You can substitute peeled and sliced apples if desired and extend the baking time for 10 minutes, until the apples are cooked. The sumac gives the tart a lovely pink-red color. We like to eat it topped with vanilla ice cream or whipped cream. ❧ **Makes one 9 x 13-inch tart**

1 pound frozen puff pastry, defrosted
1 large egg yolk, lightly beaten
¾ cup plus 2 tablespoons Dried Sumac Spice (page 193)
½ cup granulated sugar
¾ cup almond flour
6 tablespoons (¾ stick) unsalted butter, melted
16 medium Black Mission figs, sliced
2 tablespoons confectioners' sugar

1. Preheat the oven to 375°F.

2. Roll out the dough on parchment paper to fit inside an 18 × 13-inch baking sheet. Pinch the edges so that they are slightly raised. Brush the whole surface with beaten egg yolk.

3. Mix ¾ cup sumac spice, the granulated sugar, almond flour, and butter. Spread over the surface of the pastry, leaving a 1-inch border. Layer the fig slices in rows on top.

4. Bake for 10 minutes. Decrease the oven temperature to 325°F and bake for 20 minutes, or until puffed and golden on top. Remove from the oven and let cool for about 30 minutes.

5. Mix the remaining 2 tablespoons sumac spice with the confectioners' sugar and sprinkle evenly over the tart. Cut into rectangular pieces and serve.

BEACH PLUM *Prunus maritima*

Foraging level: Yellow

Form: Shrub (fruit)

Found in: Sand dunes from Maine to Maryland, as well as at local markets and festivals along the coast.

Growth habit: In groups, thickets.

Key characteristics: The plums are about the size of large grapes with a whitish bloom, and hang by a stem from the branch. Leaves are alternate and slightly toothed.

Harvest tips: The fruits ripen and turn from a magenta purple to a purple-blue color in early fall. Bring foraging buckets fashioned out of old milk containers with the tops cut off to hold the ripe fruit.

The year we had a scorching dry summer was a banner year for beach plums. I brought in a few gallons of the plums, some that were purple-blue and soft and others that were firm, almost ripe, but not squishy. Eddy loved the flavor after pressing the fruit and then cooking it as a marmalade.

Beach Plum Clafouti

A clafouti is somewhere between a cake, a custard, and a soufflé and makes for an excellent pairing with the sweet tartness of the wild beach plum. We decided to make it with the pits in, as the French do, to save the time-consuming work of pitting. Plus, the French say that leaving the pits in imparts a complex flavor and nutritional whole-someness to the dish. (For our part, my daughters had a lot of fun spitting the pits out.) This dish tasted great as a rustic dessert as well as the next morning as a special breakfast treat. 🥄 **Serves 4 to 6**

1 pound beach plums or other wild plums
½ cup granulated sugar
1 teaspoon unsalted butter, melted
3 large eggs
1 cup all-purpose flour
1¼ cups heavy cream
1 teaspoon pure vanilla extract
1 tablespoon confectioners' sugar

1. In a medium bowl, mix the beach plums with ¼ cup of the granulated sugar and let rest for 15 to 20 minutes.

2. Preheat the oven to 350°F. Grease a 10 × 10-inch baking dish with the butter.

3. In a medium bowl, beat the eggs. Add the flour, remaining ¼ cup granulated sugar, the cream, and vanilla and mix until smooth, about 3 minutes.

4. Spoon the beach plums evenly over the bottom of the baking dish and pour the batter over them and lightly mix. Bake for 35 to 45 minutes, or until golden brown on top. (You may need to increase the oven temperature to 400°F in the last 5 minutes to achieve a brown crust.) Serve warm or at room temperature, sprinkled with confectioners' sugar. It is even better if you cook it ahead of time and let it rest for more than an hour, allowing the beach plum flavors to soak into the clafouti.

PAWPAW *Asimina triloba* (SEE PHOTOGRAPH PAGE 31)

Foraging level: Red **Form:** Tree (fruit) **Found in:** Sun and part shade throughout the eastern and midwestern United States, but most common in the South. **Growth habit:** In clones that can reach from 6 to 20 feet.	**Key characteristics:** The smooth, toothless leaves can be 12 inches long, looking a bit droopy, and the flowers in spring are maroon. The fruit is the shape of a mango, first greenish and then yellow, with creamy fruit and large multiple seeds.	**Harvest tips:** Pawpaws can become pungent quickly once they begin to brown. The chefs prefer them when they are still green on the outside but the flesh yields slightly to the touch. Inside the flesh will range from creamy white to yellowish.

The first time I ever brought a pawpaw into the restaurant kitchen, Daniel's eagle eyes spied Eddy holding up a large yellow-orange tropical-looking fruit. "Where are you growing the mango?" Daniel asked. He trotted over, squeezed the fruit, and lifted it up to his nose, breathing in the faintly tropical, buttery aroma, nodding his head up and down with his eyes half-closed. When I started gleefully telling him that the pawpaw is the largest fruit growing wild in North America, his eyes opened wider and wider. Of course he had not heard of the traditional American folk song: "Pickin' up pawpaws, puttin' 'em in her pockets, Way down yonder in the pawpaw patch."

The next year, I eagerly await the day the fruit drops from my best pawpaw tree, and then rush into the downstairs prep kitchen, which is underneath the main service kitchen and is where many cooks work to prepare for the evening meal. It reminds me of a beehive down there. Every worker has a specific job, but to an observer like me it is one big bustling mass. I run into Dominique, the executive pastry chef, who greets me. "Allo, Tama! Welcome . . . to my kingdom." He gestures at all the pastry cooks around him, rolling dough, preparing delicate garnishes and chocolate confections. "You have the paa paa?" He grabs the bag and hides it away in his corner of the kitchen. "Thank you, Tama!"

Eddy spies me on my way out and says, "Allo, Tama, you have the paa paa?"

"Sorry, Dominique took all of them . . . ."

"Do-mi-NIQUE!" shouts Eddy.

Needless to say, the pawpaws are a hit, with everyone clamoring for the flavor, a cross between a mango and a banana—exotic, buttery, pungent.

Pawpaw Milkshake

This is a great treat for the whole family, plus it provides the high levels of vitamin C and other nutrients found in pawpaws. You can substitute cherimoya, a related cultivated fruit, available earlier in the summer and in specialty grocers, for the pawpaw. ❧ **Serves 6 to 8**

> 3 just-ripe pawpaws or cherimoyas (about 2 pounds)
> 1½ cups vanilla ice cream
> 30 ice cubes
> 1 cup milk
> 1 tablespoon chopped spicebush berries (optional)

1. Peel and cut each pawpaw in half; remove the large brown seeds with a spoon or your fingers. Pass the pulp through a food mill or pulse roughly in a food processor until pureed.

2. In a blender, blend the pawpaw, vanilla ice cream, ice cubes, and milk for about 3 minutes, or until smooth. Divide among individual glasses and sprinkle with the berries, if using.

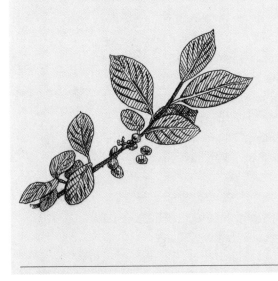

SPICEBUSH *Lindera benzoin*
Foraging level: Yellow

A native shrub found in the understory in rich, moist forests in the eastern United States, spicebush grows 5 to 15 feet tall. The alternate smooth elliptical-shaped leaves have a point on the end. Check by snapping a twig; it should have a spicy aroma, and the unripe green berries have a lemony citrus flavor. But the real treat is the oval-shaped brilliant red berries in small clusters in early autumn. The berries taste like allspice, a blend of orange and clove; they can be eaten raw or, to extend the season as the restaurant does, dried for use in small amounts to enhance fall game dishes.

Cinnamon-Spiced Pawpaw Compote with Pecans

The crunchy caramelized pecans and smooth cinnamon fruity compote make for a dynamic duo. Serve as a light dessert or, using half as much honey and sugar, add some diced cooked parsnip to accompany meat. ❧ **Serves 6**

1 tablespoon unsalted butter
1½ tablespoons honey
3 just-ripe pawpaws (about 2 pounds), peeled, halved, and seeded (about 1½ cups pulp)
3 tablespoons sugar
1 teaspoon ground cinnamon
½ cup pecans

1. In a medium saucepan, melt the butter and honey over low heat. Add the pawpaws and cook slowly for about 30 minutes, until soft.

2. Meanwhile, in a small saucepan, heat the sugar with ½ teaspoon of the cinnamon over low heat until melted. Continue to cook until the sugar turns golden, or caramelizes. Add the nuts and stir with a wooden spoon or spatula for 6 to 8 minutes, until the sugar coats the nuts. Pour out onto parchment paper, separating the nuts, and let cool. Roughly chop the nuts.

3. Pass the cooked pawpaw through a food mill or pulse in a food processor. Spoon into bowls, top with the caramelized pecans, and sprinkle with the remaining ½ teaspoon cinnamon.

WILD RAISIN *Viburnum prunifolium* (SEE PHOTOGRAPH PAGE 32)

Foraging level: Red

Form: Small tree (berry)

Found in: Edges of old fields, deciduous woods and thickets in the eastern and central United States and Canada, and also planted ornamentally. Although it is a traditional understory tree (growing under the canopy of larger trees), viburnums that are exposed to more light, on the edge of woods and in part sun, often have more berries.

Growth habit: Upright, growing to 20 feet tall.

Key characteristics: The tree has elliptical opposite leaves, about 2 inches long. The small twigs on this tree tend to grow at stiff right angles to the branches. The hard green oval berries hang down in loose umbrella-like clusters; as they ripen they turn reddish and finally blue-black.

Harvest tips: Selectively pick the berries off the tree when glossy black and slightly soft when pressed between the fingers. Dry for a day or more at room temperature, grind in a spice or coffee grinder, sieve any stems or twigs out of the powder, and store the powder in an airtight container for up to 1 year. Wild raisin is easy to plant and to care for, but be sure to distinguish it from European and other hybrid species.

There are a number of different species of viburnum, many of which bear edible fruit treasured by wildlife, but overall they are declining in the wild. The wild raisin, or blackhaw, is one of my favorites, as it was for Henry David Thoreau. He wrote that berrying for these lesser known but incredibly beautiful and sweet viburnum fruits was a favorite pastime, their taste "ever a little sweetish and raisin-like, or rather like dates." Eddy describes the wild raisin as distinctively carob and raisiny with some ending caramel notes.

Wild Raisin Crème Brûlée

Eddy chooses this smooth custard with its caramelized sugar topping as a perfect way to marry the carob and slightly caramel accents of the wild raisin. ✎ **Serves 6**

> **2 cups heavy cream**
> **1/3 cup plus 6 tablespoons (packed) light brown sugar**
> **6 large egg yolks**
> **3 tablespoons ground dried wild raisins (from about 1 cup berries)**
> **1/4 vanilla bean, split lengthwise and seeds scraped, or a few drops of pure vanilla extract**

1. Preheat the oven to 300°F. Arrange six 6- to 8-ounce shallow ramekins in a large roasting pan so they are not touching.

2. In a large bowl, using a whisk or an electric mixer on low speed, whisk the cream, 1/3 cup of the sugar, the egg yolks, wild raisin, and vanilla bean seeds until just combined. Divide among the ramekins. Carefully slide the roasting pan into the oven and pour hot water into the pan until it comes halfway up the sides of the ramekins.

3. Bake for 35 to 40 minutes, until the custard has set; when you tap a ramekin, the custard should not wiggle. Remove from the pan and cool to room temperature. Stick in the refrigerator for up to a day or two and then bring out to warm up slightly before serving.

4. When ready to serve, spread 1 tablespoon of the remaining brown sugar over the top of each ramekin. Heat the top with a cooking blowtorch (or set underneath a preheated broiler) until the sugar caramelizes. Let sit for a minute or two, until the sugar hardens, before serving.

WINTER

BARBERRY *Berberis thunbergii* (SEE PHOTOGRAPH PAGE 32)

Foraging level: Green **Form:** Shrub (berry) **Found in:** Part sun to shade in open moist woodlands in eastern and central United States and Canada. **Growth habit:** Invasive, dense stands; grows 2 to 3 feet tall.	**Key characteristics:** The teardrop or spoon-shaped leaves are smooth and clustered on the branches. At each node in the branch is a very sharp spine. The red- and sometimes orange-colored oblong fruits are $1/2$ inch long or less and hang one or two all along the twigs.	**Harvest tips:** Wait until after a heavy frost when the berries yield slightly to the touch. Cut the branches or even the entire shrub with pruning shears (the inner core will have a bright yellow color), using gloves to avoid thorns, pluck off the berries, and store in a paper bag before cooking.

The red berries of the European barberry, *Berberis vulgaris*, have been used for centuries in juice, candies, and pickles, but especially dried in Persian cuisine, served on top of rice with nuts and other fruits. Although prevalent in the United States in the early 1900s, the barberry you commonly see today is the invasive *Berberis thunbergii* (from Japan) found in moist woodlands. Unlike that species, the European barberry produces fruit in clusters at the end of the branch. I found some European barberries in early fall last year, when the berries hung in drooping pink-red clusters at the ends of the branches. Eddy loved to see it on the branch and the taste was a wonderful blend of tart and sweet, with a smooth texture, good enough to eat right off the branch.

In contrast, the Japanese barberry *Berberis thunbergii* grows rampant and in early fall is practically inedible—astringent and mealy. I know because one year, every two weeks beginning in September, I stubbornly brought Eddy samples of the berries to taste. But as the autumn chill set in, the woods turned a flame color, and after a number of hard frosts, we were rewarded. Eddy's eyebrows shot up: The taste had become sweet with a woodsy, prickly zing at the end. The texture was still poor and mealy, but that could be remedied by infusing the berries in liquids, retaining the flavor and discarding the texture. The peak time was when the berries were fully red, soft to the touch, and plump. Eddy says the taste before cooking is tart with some bitterness. Then when sugar is added, the flavor becomes sweet, almost like that of an apple.

Barberry Jelly

On New Year's Day, my husband, Wil, went out hunting pheasant at a neighbor's farm with their bird dog, Molly. Molly is a top-notch hunting dog, and Wil had an excellent catch that he prepared and then marinated in herbs and lemon. While the guys were hunting, I gathered a bagful of plump barberries for this jelly (I made sure to wear red and orange so I would not be inadvertently mistaken for game). The sweet juiciness of this runny barberry jelly paired excellently with the lean, dry, lemon herb quality of the game meat. It's also lovely over rice pudding for dessert. ❧ **Makes 2 cups**

> 1 cup ripe Japanese barberries, slightly soft to the touch,
>   picked after the first frost
> 1 cup sugar
> 1 tablespoon fresh lemon juice
> 1 (1³/₄-ounce) package powdered pectin

1. Put the berries in a medium pot with 2 cups water, bring to a boil over high heat, and boil for 5 minutes. Remove from the heat and let steep for 1 hour.

2. Strain the liquid through a jelly bag or cheesecloth for 3 to 5 hours, wringing to extract a maximum of the clear red juice and discarding the solids. Set a small plate in the freezer for testing the jelly later. Transfer the liquid to a large saucepan, bring to a boil, and add the sugar, ½ cup at a time, and the lemon juice, returning to a boil.

3. In a heat-safe 1-cup measure, vigorously mix the pectin with ¼ cup of the hot liquid so that the pectin does not become lumpy. Add the pectin mixture to the pan and boil for 3 minutes. Check the consistency by dropping a teaspoon of the hot jelly onto the chilled plate and leaving it in the freezer for 10 seconds. When you run a finger through the gel on the plate it should form a trail or otherwise achieve the consistency you are looking for. If it does not, continue to boil for 2 more minutes. Remove from the heat. Pour into jelly jars and refrigerate.

Wild Barberry Rice Pudding

This pudding makes a great winter holiday dessert with its jewel-like red and cream colors. The light fluffiness of the sweet rice pudding pairs nicely with the barberry's full-bodied wild flavor with hints of cranberry. You can prepare this ahead of time, keeping it in the refrigerator and taking it out an hour before serving. ✒ **Serves 4 to 6**

RICE PUDDING
$1/2$ **cup short-grain or sushi rice**
3$1/2$ cups whole milk
7 tablespoons heavy cream
$1/2$ **cup sugar**
Pinch of salt
1 teaspoon vanilla extract

BARBERRY COULIS
1$1/2$ cups ripe barberries
1 cup sugar

CUSTARD
1 cup whole milk
$1/2$ **cup heavy cream**
$1/2$ **teaspoon vanilla extract**
4 large egg yolks
$1/4$ **cup sugar**

1. To make the rice pudding, preheat the oven to 300°F.

2. Rinse the rice by submerging it in a bowl of cold water, swishing it around, and draining. Repeat twice.

3. In a large ovenproof saucepan, heat the milk and cream, stirring in the sugar, salt, and vanilla. As the mixture begins to simmer, add the rice. Cover the pan and transfer to the oven for 1 hour until the rice is cooked and has absorbed the liquid. Remove the lid and set aside to cool.

4. To make the barberry coulis, in a medium saucepan combine the barberries and sugar with ¾ cup water and bring to a boil. Reduce the heat to medium and simmer for 10 to 15 minutes, or until softened and the liquid is a jewel-like red color. Remove from the heat and set aside to cool. Pass through a food mill or strainer to remove the black seeds. Be sure to press through as much of the pulp as possible so that the coulis is nice and thick.

5. To make the custard, heat the milk, cream, and vanilla in a medium saucepan over medium heat until nearly boiling. Meanwhile, in a medium bowl, whisk together the egg yolks and sugar until well combined. Slowly pour half of the hot milk mixture into the egg mixture, whisking to combine, and then pour everything back into the saucepan. Stir with a wooden spoon over medium-low heat for 2 to 3 minutes, or until thickened. Do not boil or the mixture will curdle. Remove from the heat, pour into a heatproof bowl, and cool completely in the refrigerator.

6. Mix the custard with the rice. Spoon half of the mixture into 4 to 6 individual serving dishes (such as ramekins or martini glasses), add a dollop of barberry coulis, and top with the remaining pudding. Serve immediately or refrigerate overnight.

WHITE PINE *Pinus strobus* (SEE PHOTOGRAPH PAGE 31)

Foraging level: Green **Form: Tree (needles)** **Found in: Eastern and central United States (excluding Florida) and Canada; also common in landscape plantings. The western United States boasts the ponderosa pine as well as the western white pine.**	**Growth habit: Upright, conical when young and becoming flat-topped as it matures, reaching heights of 150 feet.** **Key characteristics: Five long, slender needles in each bundle or cluster attached to the twig.**	**Harvest tips: Cut branches in winter and early spring when you can clearly smell the pine sap aroma. Choose thinner needle clusters as they will crumble most easily.**

The pine is symbolic in Japan for its lasting nature. It is said that pines do not change their colors and remain friends for a thousand years. I tried soaking some white pine needles in hot water over the winter holidays and the aroma reminded me of Pine-Sol. I made one of the girls taste it and her response was, "Blechhhh." So I brought pine needles to Eddy only because he was once again bugging me about "what is out there now" since the local farmer's markets didn't have much fresh produce that time of year. He pulled a branch out of the bag and examined it, sniffing. There was not much aroma since I had cut it when it was 15 degrees out. But he surprised me with his reaction—to try to roast them and make a bed for some fish. He had once eaten mussels roasted on top of pine needles over an open fire. I never thought of that.

I have dinner with business colleagues that evening at the restaurant. A casserole dish arrives at the table: turbot resting on a bed of pine branches. On top of the fish are individual toasted pine needles that taste like little toasty sesame sticks that melt in your mouth. Eddy added toasted pine nuts, so there is this very mild complexity of the nuts with the needles. On top of the fish are roasted porcini mushrooms with a rich sauce. The rich heartiness and juiciness of the mushrooms balance the dryness of the pine; the turbot is mild and moist. The next week we have fun re-creating the dish at home, baking the white fish in the oven on top of pine branches and toasting the pine needles separately so we can crumble them over the dish with a portobello mushroom sauce. Definitely a keeper.

Pine Needle Oil

Aromatic and good as a base for a dressing or for brushing on grilled or roasted fish or chicken. ❧ **Makes 1 cup**

> 3 ounces (4 cups) aromatic pine needles (from three 2-foot pine branches), dried at room temperature for 1 day
> 2 teaspoons salt
> 2 teaspoons red pepper flakes
> 1 cup grapeseed or canola oil

In a coffee or spice grinder, working in batches, blend the pine needles to a powder with the salt and red pepper flakes. In a pint jar, stir the powder into the oil. Store in the refrigerator for up to a month.

FORAGER'S JOURNAL

During a week-long power outage in our community recently, everyone helped out one another. One neighbor brought us gasoline for our emergency generator and also shared some tips and pointers on "living off the grid." It turns out he has really been studying up on preparing for emergencies, and is especially concerned about food-supply shortages. While he has a store of canned and dry food on hand, just in case, he jumped eagerly when I told him about foraging for wild food. I gave him some delicious toasted pine needles for the fish dinner he was planning that night. Now he says he will bring us gasoline anytime in exchange for wild foods.

JUNIPER: EASTERN RED CEDAR *Juniperus virginiana*

(SEE PHOTOGRAPH PAGE 31)

Foraging level: Yellow

Form: Tree (berries, needles)

Found in: Sunny fields, hedgerows, and open spaces in the eastern and central United States and Canada; substitute western juniper in other parts of the country.

Growth habit: Upright, dense and slow growing, reaching 20 to 60 feet tall.

Key characteristics: Evergreen with waxy bluish to black berries on branches with flat needles; only female plants have berries.

Harvest tips: Choose a few branches in fall or winter when they are laden with ripe gray-blue (not green) berries and cut selectively close to where the berries join the branch. Pluck the berries. Dry in a warm dry place indoors using a home dehydrator or in an oven set to its lowest temperature. Once dried, the skin starts to wrinkle a bit. Store in an airtight container. Grind in a spice or coffee grinder just before using.

French cuisine has long prized the dark, almost black, dried berries of *Juniperus communis*, or juniper, one of the most widespread evergreens in the world. So when Jean-François asked me to bring him juniper for game dishes in the fall, I thought, what could be easier? But it was not so simple. Common juniper is mostly found on rocky or cliff edges and only the female trees bear berries—which are really cones that can take years to turn from green to blue or black. I could not envision myself clinging to the side of a ledge on the chance that I might find a couple of stray unripe berries. So instead of the "common" juniper I turned to easier-to-find junipers: eastern red cedar (which is really *Juniperus virginiana*) and *Juniperus chinensis*, Chinese juniper, a widely used landscape plant that has larger berries and an even stronger taste, which some people prefer.

I brought in branches laden with the waxy bluish berries. Jean-François said the berries were not as dark as he was used to. But after he bit down fiercely into the Chinese juniper berry, he nodded his approval of its strong woodsy and even slight ammonia-like aroma. Eddy prefers working with the less pungent eastern red cedar, *Juniperus virginiana*, and describes the taste as woodsy and piney, like walking through a forest and breathing in a sharp, crisp aroma.

The essential oil of juniper can be powerful medicinally and folk remedies have used it in larger doses as a diuretic to increase kidney filtration and stimulate childbirth. Therefore, cooking it as an infusion or drying and grinding small amounts of berries or needles (i.e., the traditional French way) is recommended.

Caramelized Braised Endive with Juniper Berries

The juniper aroma is very subtle in this dish where the sharp, woodsy berry flavor balances that of the meltingly soft endive. You first taste the sweetness and tenderness of the caramelized endive; then the juniper flavor lingers at the end. This is a nice accompaniment to game or Thanksgiving turkey. ❧ **Serves 4**

> **4 medium Belgian endives**
> **4 tablespoons (½ stick) unsalted butter**
> **1 tablespoon ground dried eastern red cedar juniper berries, plus more for serving**
> **1 tablespoon sugar**
> **Salt and freshly ground black pepper**

1. Preheat the oven to 325°F.

2. Remove the outer leaves and cut away the tough bottom from each endive. Melt the butter in a small heavy ovenproof skillet over medium-low heat, add the endives, and sprinkle with the juniper and sugar. Season with salt and pepper. Cook, turning them gently after the color changes on one side, for about 25 minutes, or until the outside edges turn a medium caramel-brown.

3. Cover the skillet and transfer to the oven for about 45 minutes. The endive should turn a deeper chocolate color but still be soft and melty. Sprinkle with a pinch of ground juniper before serving.

Sweet and Sour Daikon Radish with Crushed Juniper Berries

In the winter months, Asian cuisine boasts a lot of pickled side dishes, both as a way to preserve the harvest and also for health. Here the sweet and sour notes of pickled radish get a woodsy boost from the juniper berry. The addition of sweet carrot as well as salty ham make this more than just a condiment. Pair it, as one would sauerkraut, with pork chops or grilled fish as a side dish. ❧ **Serves 4**

> 1 large or 2 medium white daikon radishes (1¼ pounds),
>   peeled and very thinly sliced into shreds or coins
> 4 teaspoons sugar
> 1 cup rice vinegar
> ½ cup mirin
> ⅓ cup dry white wine, optional
> 2 sprigs fresh thyme
> 1 bay leaf
> 2½ tablespoons dried Eastern red cedar juniper berries
> 2 tablespoons olive oil
> 5 ounces speck ham or Canadian or smoked bacon, diced
> 1½ garlic cloves
> 3 medium carrots, cut into ½-inch diced
> ½ medium onion, diced
> 2 cups chicken stock
> Pinch of red pepper flakes
> Salt
> Pinch of ground dried juniper berries, plus more for serving

1. In a large nonreactive bowl, combine the daikon with the sugar, vinegar, mirin, and white wine, if using. Put the juniper berries, thyme, and bay leaf in a tea strainer (or tie them in a double layer of cheesecloth) and add to the bowl. Let marinate in the refrigerator for 2 hours or up to 1 day.

2. In a large saucepan, heat the olive oil over medium heat and add the ham. Cook, stirring occasionally, until lightly browned, about 5 minutes. Add the carrots and onion and cook for about 2 minutes.

3. Strain the liquid from the radish and discard the liquid. Add the radish and spice sachet to the pan. Cook for 5 minutes. Pour in the chicken stock and red pepper flakes, season with salt, and cover the pan. Simmer over low heat for about 45 minutes or until the liquid has almost evaporated.

4. When serving, sprinkle the ground juniper over the dish to taste.

Acknowledgments

One of the great pleasures in life is to work together with a team of imaginative, expert, and practical people whom you admire and respect. And so this book is the fruit of just such a collaboration among very diverse people, tied up in a bow with a flash of good timing.

EDDY:

I wish to give my sincere thanks to:

Daniel Boulud, for giving me the best opportunity of my life. His culinary passion and hospitality are second to none. His endless energy and dedication make him my role model.

Tama Matsuoka, who has been challenging me with the hundreds of plants she has brought in for the last two and a half years, for her passion and dedication to a better, more sustainable way of life.

Jean-François Bruel, our veteran executive chef at Daniel, who remains the pillar of the "brigade"; the talented chefs at Daniel: Gregory Stawowy and Yun Young Lee, Eric Bertoia, Dominique Ansel, Roger Ma, Sebastien Mathieu, Colin Wyatt, Devin Broo, Tyler Shedden, Soo Gil, Brian Loiacono, Anna McGorman, and the rest of the team of taste testers.

Joel Buchman, our loyal devotee at restaurant Daniel.

Monsieur et Madame Senderens, for laying the foundation of my journeys in the culinary world.

Laurent Gras, my most influential mentor, for polishing my skills.

And for balance in my life, my lovely wife, Fati, for her patience and endless support for my passion.

My late father and grandfather, who made my dreams of being a chef possible.

My mum, for her love and for tolerating the mess in her kitchen while I was experimenting.

TAMA:

I also thank and love the team in the Daniel kitchen, with their incredible buzz and brilliant talent, many of whom are captured in the pages of this book, working hard under the vision and nurturing eye of Daniel Boulud. A big thanks, too, to the front-of-the-house staff at Daniel to whom both Eddy and I are so very grateful for embracing this project and for their sincerity, charm, salty wit, and hard work, including Pierre Siue and his entire team, especially Elvir Dzananovic, John Winterman, Melissa Termyna, Liz Rodriguez, Kevin Crow, Rajeev Vaidya, Pascal Vittu, Xavier Herit, Joan Chiang, and Staci Chen. A very special thanks to Ginette, Bernard, and Yannick Vrod whom I look forward to seeing every week and exchanging tales of plants found, of fishing and hunting. Thanks also to Miguel Vaja in the prep kitchen who, sometimes chuckling nervously, cleaned up a lot of the strange things I brought in. Georgette Farkas and Maisie Wilhelm, thank you also for your support, help, and incredible expertise.

In my family, thanks to my mother, for imparting to me her joy in puttering around in the garden and as the ultimate New Age Hawaiian weed forager, back in the day; to my father, the logical scientist, with his delight of all things *wabi-sabi*, and its celebration of beauty that is impermanent and asymmetrical; to my husband, Wil, and our three daughters for their daily encouragement, sound advice, laughter, cooking, and just plain mucking about; and to my in-laws, Harry and Ivy Wong, for their dedication to family and very good eating.

To Leslie Sauer, for being the first to enlighten me that all green plants are not the same ecologically, and Dr. Gerould Wilhelm, for further enthralling me with both the scientific classifications and the lyrical nature of plants. William Wyman, Bill Rawlyk, Jeannine Vannais, Mark Gallagher, Les Alpaugh, and the naturalists at Bowmans Hill Wildflower Preserve, for sharing incessant questions and obsessive plant talk. Foraging and farming companions Tim Stark, Larry Rossi, Anita and Jim Lau, the guys at Comeback Farms, Michael Van Clef, Kyla Chasalow, and Mia Wong.

To Elisa and Richard Rosen, for introducing us to restaurant Daniel in the first place, and urging me to bring in a meadow plant before dinner.

To Melissa Hamilton, for teaching and introducing me to the world of food professionals, cookbookery, and recipe testing, and for her fierce dedication to the craft and keeping it all real.

To Jean Lynch, for astonishing me by believing this project was book worthy, from whom I first heard the name Clarkson Potter, which ultimately led to the book proposal finding its best home. To Steve Levicky, for his dedication to creating our website and Meadows and More design.

To dear friends Jean Hwang Carrant, Kathryn Tsang, Deborah Agnew, Troy Ettel, and Marie Newell, for jogging along beside me on the book's path with encouragement, invaluable advice, and more than a couple of laughs.

And to Eddy Leroux, for his fearlessness in taking on this "plant challenge," and for those qualities I most admire in my close friends: his curiosity and his humility. Thank you for believing in the plants from the beginning and for always sticking with us.

TOGETHER:

Our thanks to the fantastic team that put together this book:

Sharon Bowers, our spirited and indefatigable agent, for shepherding us through the world of cookbooks and publishing.

Karl Anderson, field botanist par excellence and trusted adviser.

My enthusiastic yet disarmingly honest home testers: Lynne Federman and Georgia Wong, Richard Rosen, and John Parke. And to Rebecca Wong, home editor and critic.

Rica Allannic, our very smart and talented editor, thank you for believing in this book and for keeping us from debating ingredients and techniques ad infinitum. And to the entire team at Clarkson Potter—including Marysarah Quinn, Ashley Phillips, Ada Yonenaka, Kim Tyner, and Derek Gullino—for transforming our Word document into a symphony, and for their dedication, gorgeous design, and patience with this, our first-time writing collaboration.

Thomas Schauer and Sahinaz, for capturing the natural beauty of the wild plants and for going above and beyond to find the last flowering multiflora rose in the woods.

Kate McKeon, for your lovely illustrations and winningly professional ways.

Lastly, we wish to express our gratefulness to conservation groups and all others who steward the land to care for wild plants—who are after all the true stars of this endeavor.

Resources

I encourage you to consult my website for additional resources and information, including plant identification assistance, field and food photos, and nursery and online sources: www.meadowsandmore.com.

FIELD GUIDES

Newcomb's Wildflower Guide (Lawrence Newcomb, Little Brown, 1989) is a classic used by nonbotanists in the field, although it is somewhat outdated and has a focus on flowers when in bloom.

Weeds of the Northeast (Richard Hart Uva, Joseph Crowell Neal, and Joseph M. DiTomaso, Comstock Publishing Associates, 1997) is a useful introduction to common weeds with photos of the plant when at basal rosette stage as well as growth habit in the field before flowering. Although the title says "of the Northeast," many of the weeds are found throughout North America.

The United States Department of Agriculture plants database has more than 40,000 plant images and a general map of where the plant can be found in the United States and Canada. You need to know the species name to accurately search the database: www.plants.usda.gov/java/.

Every state has a county Cooperative Extension office for information on natural resources and the environment. See www.csrees.usda.gov/extension/.

Contact your local conservation group or chapter of Slow Food, the National Audubon Society, watershed organization, or local botanical garden for more information.

The Book of Field and Roadside: Open-Country Weeds, Trees, and Wildflowers of Eastern North America (John Eastman and Amelia Hansen, Stackpole Books, 2003) is part of a series of books that can serve as an identification field guide but also give a more holistic view of the ecological associations between featured plants and the wildlife community.

GUIDES TO BACKYARD NATURE AND ECOLOGY

Bringing Nature Home: How You Can Sustain Wildlife with Native Plants (Douglas W. Tallamy, Timber Press, 2007).

Noah's Garden: Restoring the Ecology of Our Own Backyards (Sara Stein, Houghton Mifflin, 1995).

Last Child in the Woods: Saving Our Children from Nature-Deficit Disorder (Richard Louv, Algonquin Books, 2008).

For further information on sustainability levels of plants in your state, consult my website or Bowman's Hill Wildflower Preserve (www.bhwp.org) regarding the Plant Stewardship Index or Floristic Quality Assessment Index (FQAI) developed by Floyd Swink and Gerould Wilhelm.

FOOD

The Encyclopedia of Edible Plants of North America (Francois Couplan, Keats Publishing, 1998).

Identifying and Harvesting Edible and Medicinal Plants in Wild (and Not So Wild) Places (Steven Brill, Harper Paperbacks, 1994).

The Omnivore's Dilemma (Michael Pollan, Penguin Press, 2006).

Slow Food Nation (Carlo Petrini, Rizzoli, 2007).

Stalking the Wild Asparagus (Euell Gibbons, Alan C. Hood & Co., 1962).

The Plants for a Future website based in the United Kingdom compiles a database of 7,000 plant species for which they have found some record of edible or medicinal use: www.pfaf.org.

About the Authors

TAMA MATSUOKA WONG is the forager for the restaurant Daniel in New York City and enjoys relationships with organizations that include the Audubon Society and Slow Food. After more than twenty-five years as a financial-services lawyer, she launched Meadows and More, LLC, to connect experts in the fields of meadow restoration, botany, and wildlife with people in the community. In 2007, she was named Steward of the Year by the New Jersey Forest Service. Visit her at www.MeadowsandMore.com.

EDDY LEROUX is the chef de cuisine at Daniel, the award-winning flagship restaurant of celebrity chef Daniel Boulud.

Index

Boldfaced page numbers indicate photographs.